Annette Feldman **The Needlework Boutique**

Rutledge Books
New York

Dedicated
in Loving Memory to My Parents,
Gertrude and Emanuel Gerber,
and to
My Husband, Irving,
and
My Boys, Arnold H., Murray L., and Richard A.

Published in 1977 by Rutledge Books,
25 West 43 Street, New York, N.Y. 10036.
Copyright 1977 in all countries of the
International Copyright Union by Rutledge
Books, a division of Arcata Consumer Products
Corporation. All rights reserved.
Printed in Italy by Mondadori, Verona.

Distributed by Charles Scribner's Sons, New York, N.Y.

Library of Congress Cataloging in Publication Data

Feldman, Annette.
    The needlework boutique.

    Includes index.
    1.   Needlework.   I.   Title.
TT750.F44   746.4   77-7061
ISBN 0-87469-012-9

CONTENTS

INTRODUCTION

In the planning of the rather unusual boutique that appears within the pages of this book, our guiding thought has been to offer you a group of little things that would please you to make, either for yourself or as a special gift for someone else. Often in the course of doing this, fond memories have come to us of those days before there were "boutiques," and even beyond then to days when we were very young and when the enjoyment of buying a few small special things that pleased us contributed a great deal toward making some of the happier experiences of our lives.

Good memories for many of us go back to when a stop at the neighborhood candy store with a few loose pennies jangling in our pocket was probably one of the major events of our day. It used to take us a long time, perhaps even the longer the better, to be able to decide just which of the tempting confections pleased us the most. Very often our choice would finally turn out to be a piece of Turkish taffy, maybe even one layered with peanut butter and certainly one sufficiently chewy to last long enough to make our investment a worthwhile one. And those among us who were more affluent probably recall having often hovered for quite some time in deep concentration on the outside of a bakery shop, savoring the sight of everything on display, almost tasting it all through the plate-glass window, and then finally going inside to make the very satisfying purchase of either a big, round jelly doughnut that oozed with pitted red raspberry jam from the very first bite to the last or perhaps, better yet, a chocolate-coated eclair that lay on a tray, along with many others, ready to spurt rich sweet custard from all sides at that moment when it became our own, about to be devoured.

And we remembered too how, when we grew older, our interest seemed to shift away from the candy store and the bakery shop on to the counters of the five-and-ten laden with toys and trinkets that we needed to have. We would dawdle for many hours in these places too, and always we took a great deal of time in making one selection or another, which we would play with until eventually it broke or we outgrew it, and then we would go on to other things.

Now, for most of us, new little pleasures have taken the place of our early temptations, although many of those we share today bear close resemblance to those earlier ones, especially our love for browsing around one display or another of attractive little things, several of which we would like to taste, or touch, or try on. Practically all of us enjoy attending a country fair or idling through the various shops in the local mall, and few of us ever leave these places without having been tempted to buy something that seems to hold special interest and appeal for us, some small thing, perhaps, that's just a little different from anything else that we already have. In the same way, one of our most exciting small pleasures now is to wander through one or another interesting boutique, the relatively new type of establishment in this country specializing in trinkets, accessories, and gifts, many of them the kind of items from which new excitement in fashion is generated.

The entrance to the average boutique is usually through the doors of a small shop in some fashionable area of town; it is indeed a little different to be able to enter one through the pages of a book, as you are about to do now. Our special boutique here, right in your hands, is filled with pages rather than counters, and our pages are covered with many attractive things for all of us for our personal pleasure and for the delight of those we know and love, including our friends, our children, and even our pets. You will find in our Pet Toggery, for instance, a smart patchwork denim coat for your dog, a chic turtleneck mohair sweater to keep your cat warm on cold winter nights, and a personalized bird-cage cover to let that one enjoy quiet, sweet dreams while he sits attractively sheltered away from the lights and the sounds of those outside his cage. In other chapters, there are attractive cord espadrilles for ladies, a big turtle called Terrance and flying birds and a dancing gingerbread mobile for the delight of little children, and even a stunning striped necktie for him, Scotch plaid golf club covers with numbers marked out in bright red ball-fringe for anyone who enjoys the game, and a small Oriental wall hanging to add interest to your home.

And our shop differs in just one more way. Nothing in it can be bought; you have to make whatever it is you want. The "you" enters into all the charming things displayed on these pages. Your hands can create any or all of the items shown. This is perhaps the most important attraction of our special boutique—handwork, your own creation, which adds a priceless tag to anything made besides offering you an opportunity to enjoy the very gratifying experience of being able to produce something beautiful with a personal touch. You can choose your own craft to work in, for there are some projects for knitting and some for crocheting; others for needlepoint and latchet-hook work, and hairpin lace and macramé. Experienced workers will find everything here quite simple to make; and for one just venturing into the world of needlecraft, or wanting to experiment with a new craft, there are complete, easy-to-follow "how-to" instructions given in the last chapter that leave no step in any project unexplained.

It is our hope that you will enjoy your visit to our boutique and that you will find as much delight in trying our designs as you perhaps found long ago in trying the many creations of the local candy, pastry, or trinket shop.

ALPHABET CHART

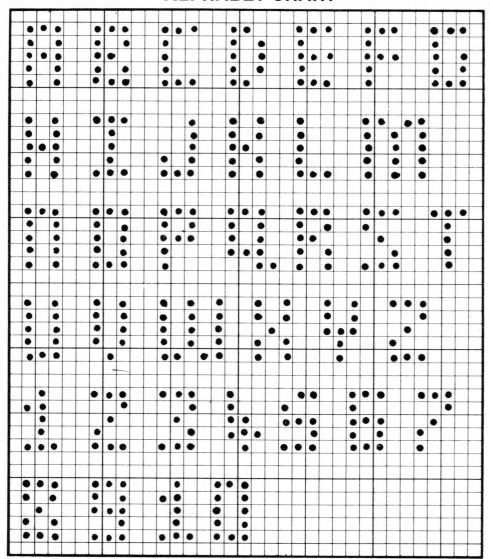

ABBREVIATIONS

beg	beginning	psso	pass slip stitch over
ch	chain	pat	pattern
CC	contrast color	p	purl
dec	decrease	rep	repeat
dc	double crochet	rnd	round
dp	double point	sc	single crochet
dbl tr	double treble	sk	skip
hdc	half double crochet	sl	slip
inc	increase	sl st	slip stitch
k	knit	sp(s)	space(s)
lp(s)	loop(s)	st(s)	stitch(es)
MC	main color	tog	together
		tr c	treble crochet

1

the needlework boutique

The Children's Hour

Opposite, from left to right: *Terrance, the Turtle,*
p. 23; Gingerbread Boy Jamboree, p. 18; The
Friendly Puppets, p. 15; A Learn-to-Count Chart,
p. 12; Hide 'n Seek Gingerbread Toy, p. 21. Above,
from left to right: *Tree of Life Sampler, p. 26;*
Bluebird Ballet, p. 29; The Delicate Air: A Soft and
Simple Child's Shawl, p. 32.

1
A Learn-to-Count Chart

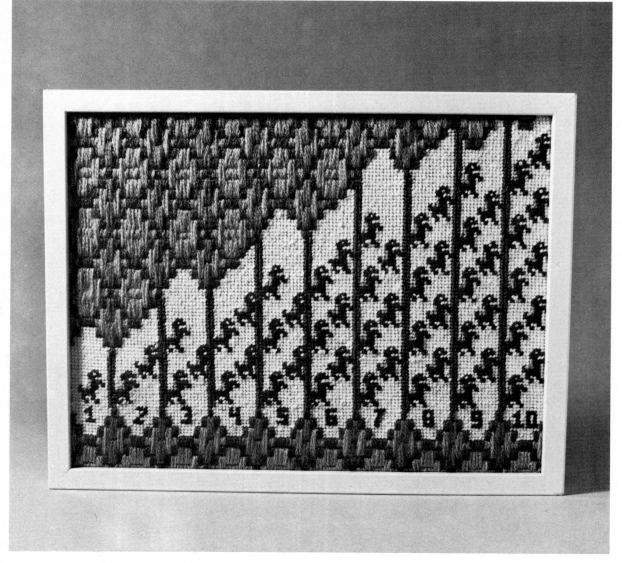

Dancing puppies introduce toddlers to the shapes of numerals and give them a head start on learning to count via this bright needlepoint picture. A simple bargello stitch forms the colorful asymmetrical border. Use a yarn in the child's favorite color to make the border, and if he has a pet dog, substitute the pet's fur color for brown when stitching the puppies in the picture. The finished picture measures 10½ by 13 inches, and it takes only about fifteen hours to complete.

Materials:

28 skeins (8.8 yards each) Paragon 3-ply Persian Yarn: 7 skeins in off-white
#740, 7 skeins in deep green #712, 7 skeins in light green #714, 5
skeins in medium green #713, and 2 skeins in medium brown #617
needlepoint canvas, 10 mesh to an inch, 13 × 16 inches
masking tape
tapestry needle: #18

The Counting Chart

Bind the edges of the canvas with masking tape. Leaving 10 rows of mesh
(1 inch) unworked around all four edges of the canvas and starting to work
at the lower right-hand corner, follow the stitch and color keys to completion
of the piece.

Finishing: Block the piece, turn the four unworked edges to the wrong side
of the work, and then mount or frame the piece as desired.

COLOR and STITCH KEY

Continental Stitch:

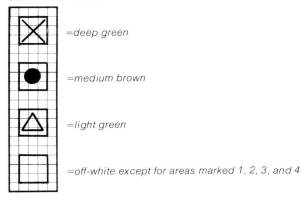

=deep green

=medium brown

=light green

=off-white except for areas marked 1, 2, 3, and 4

Gobelin Stitch:

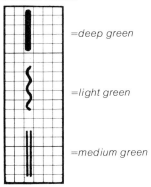

=deep green

=light green

=medium green

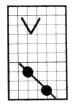

=off-white French knot

=long medium brown continental stitch worked in reverse to the
others under the two continental stitches forming each paw

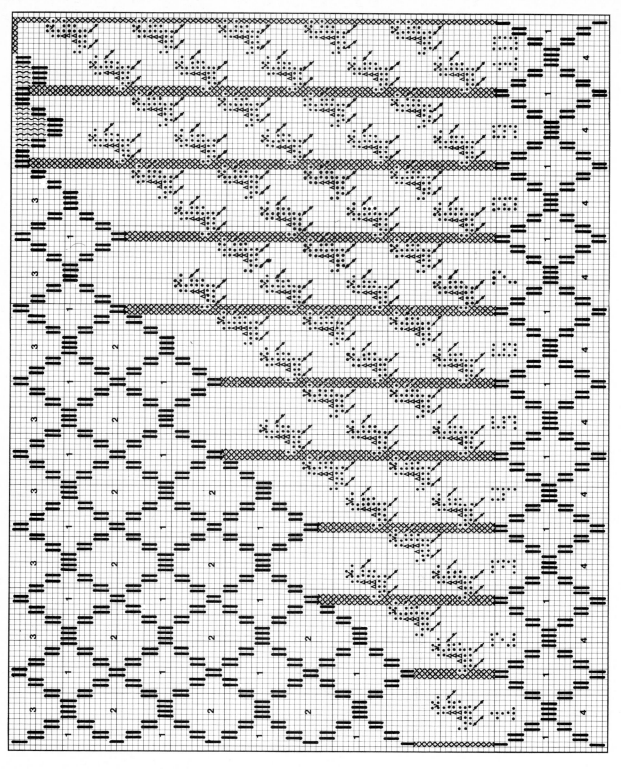

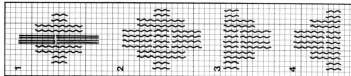

14

2
The Friendly Puppets

These grinning hand puppets will draw big smiles from children and grown-ups alike as they wave, clap, talk, and dance. Bright colors make these puppets merry, and Speed-Cro-Sheen makes them light and flexible to play with. Their details aren't complicated but the results are endearing playmates. The boy is gaily outfitted in a red-and-white striped polo shirt and jeans. The clown has a collar ruffle, a cuffed hat, and perfect clown makeup. A full shock of hair bursts from their heads. The size is a happy compromise that accommodates an adult's hand and isn't too big for a kid to handle, either.

Materials:

5 balls Coats & Clark's "Speed-Cro-Sheen": 1 ball each in nu-ecru (A), canary yellow (B), medium blue (C), spanish red (D), peach (E), and small amounts of black (F) and white (G), for both puppets

aluminum crochet hook: size D

tapestry needle: #18

Gauge in Single Crochet: 5 stitches = 1 inch

The Clown

Suit: Starting at the bottom with Color B for one half of the front and back of the clown's suit, ch 26 and work in sc on 25 sts for 4 inches. Continuing in sc throughout, work as follows: Sc across the first 13 sts, ch 6 for the sleeve, turn. *Next Row:* Sc in the 2nd ch from hook and in each of the next 4 ch; then work across the remaining 13 sts. Work even now on 18 sts for 1½ inches, ending at the front edge. *Next Row:* Sl st across 9 sts, work across the remaining 9 sts, and fasten off. With another piece of B, ch 5; then work 1 sc in the 1st sc on the row where the sts were added for the shaping of the sleeve and in each of the remaining 12 sc, ch 1, and turn. Work even now on this group of 18 sts for 1½ inches, and finish as for the first part, reversing the shaping. Using Color A, work another piece to correspond to the Color B piece but reversing the shaping. *Finishing:* Sew the shoulder and sleeve seams; then sew the Color A half of the suit to the B half down the centers of both the front and the back. Then with A, work 25 sc around the neck opening, easing in any extra fullness on the 1st rnd. Finally, work 1 rnd even.

Head (Make two pieces): With E, ch 2; then work 6 sc in the 2nd ch from hook. *Next Rnd:* Work 2 sc in each sc around (12 sc). Add a marker to denote the start of next and all following rnds. *Next Rnd:* *Work 1 sc in the 1st sc, 2 sc in the next sc, rep from * around (18 sc). *Next Rnd:* *Work 1 sc in each of the next 2 sc, 2 sc in the next sc, rep from * around (24 sc). Continue in this manner to inc 6 sts evenly spaced on each rnd, allowing on each rnd 1 st more between each point of increase until there are 54 sc in all. Join last rnd with a sl st and fasten off.

Hat (Make two pieces, one with Color A and one with Color B): Ch 16 and work 1 row even on 15 sts. Then dec 1 st at beg and end of the next row and every row thereafter until 1 st remains. Fasten off. Sew the Color A and Color B parts of the hat together. Then with the wrong side of the piece facing and working with A, work 30 sc around the bottom edge for 4 rnds. Break off A, attach C, work 1 more rnd, and fasten off.

Hands (Make four pieces): With E, ch 7; then work even in sc on 6 sts for 4 rows, ch 1, and turn. *Next Row:* Sc across 3 sts, ch 1, and turn. *Next Row:* Sc in 1st st, sl st across each of the next 2 sts, and fasten off.

Nose: With D, ch 2. Work 5 sc in the 2nd ch from hook, and then work 2 sc in each sc. Work 2 rows even on 10 sts and fasten off.

Mouth: With G, ch 14. Work 1 sc in the 2nd ch from hook and in each of the next 11 ch; work 3 sc in the last ch. Then work in sc across the opposite side of the chain, ending with 2 sc in the 1st sc. Join the piece with a sl st in the 1st sc. Fasten off.

Ruff: With A, ch 31. Work 1 sc in the 2nd ch from hook and in each ch across row, ch 1, and turn. *Next Row:* *Ch 4, sl st in the next sc, rep from * across. Work in the same manner across the opposite side of the chain and fasten off. Work 1 row of Color C around the ruff as follows: Attach yarn in the 1st ch-4 sp, *ch 3, sl st in the next sp, rep from * around, and fasten off. In the same way, work another Color C rnd on the opposite side of the ruff.

Buttons and Hat Pom-Pom (Make four pieces): With C, ch 2. Work 5 sc in the 2nd ch from hook and then 2 sc in each sc around. Fasten off.

Finishing: Stuff the nose lightly and sew it to the center of one of the head pieces. With D and a small running stitch, embroider a line on the mouth, as shown in the photograph. Sew the mouth in position and then, with F, embroider an outline stitch around the piece. With four strands of C, embroider an X for each eye; with F, embroider a small running stitch for each eyebrow. Sew the trimmed head piece to the other head piece, right sides out. Turn up the brim of the hat and sew the piece to the top of the head. Now sew the head to the open neck portion of the suit piece. Sew one of the small Color C circles to the top of the hat. Sew the ruff around the neck portion of the suit. Using Color C, work 1 row of sc around each sleeve edge; then sew the two parts of each hand together, insert the finished hands into the sleeves, and sew them in place. Trim the front of the suit with the three remaining small Color C buttons. Cut strands of Color D yarn for the hair, each measuring 2½ inches, and trim each side of the face by knotting them into the stitches, as shown in the project photograph.

The Boy

Body (Make two pieces): Starting at the bottom with Color C, ch 26. Work in sc on 25 sts for 2 inches. Break off C, attach A, and, working in sc to completion now, alternate 2 rows A and 2 rows D twice. Then work 2 more rows of A. Drop A and, working with D, ch 5 for one sleeve, work across the 25 body sts, ch 6 at the end of the row for the other sleeve, and turn. Continuing with D, work 1 more row across the 35 sts. Then work 2 rows A, 2 rows D, and 2 rows A. On the next row, working with D, sc across 9 sts, sl st across 17 sts for the neck, and sc across the remaining 9 sts for the other shoulder. Fasten off. Sew the side, shoulder, and sleeve seams. With D, work 25 sc around the neck opening, easing in any extra fullness on that rnd, and then work 1 more rnd even on the 25 sc.

Head (Make two pieces): Work as for the head on the clown.

Hands (Make two pieces): Work as for the hands on the clown.

Eyes (Make two pieces): With C, ch 2 and then work a sc, dc, and sc in the 2nd ch from hook; fasten off.

Finishing: With double strands of F, embroider a cross stitch for the nose on one of the head pieces and a small V in the corner of each eye; sew the eyes in place. Still using F, embroider eyebrows with an outline stitch; with D, embroider a small mouth, as shown in the project photograph. Sew the two pieces for the head together, right sides out, and then sew the completed head to the neck opening. With D, work 1 row of sc around each sleeve edge; then join the hands as for the clown's hands, and sew them in place at the sleeve edges. Cut strands of Color B yarn for the hair, each measuring 2½ inches, and knot two strands in each stitch around the sides and top of the head, as shown in the project photograph, knotting a double row of fringe along the top of the head for bangs.

3
Gingerbread Boy Jamboree

This mobile's meant to provide lots of smiles. The stuffed gingerbread boys, dancing from the inside ring of an embroidery hoop and bright-colored wooden beads, are happy companions to the Hide 'n Seek Gingerbread Toy shown in this chapter. The stitch directions for all four men are the same—you simply use larger crochet hooks to make the bigger ones. "Raisin" buttons and "cherry" smiles add to the gaiety, as does the bright yellow "neckwear" the toys sport. In just an evening's time, you can have this project ready to hang over a crib and fascinate baby for hours.

Materials:

2 balls (1 ounce each) Spinnerin Frostlon Petite in rust (MC)
small amounts of lightweight yarn in black (A), medium blue (B), and red (C)
4 aluminum crochet hooks: sizes B, E, G, and H
tapestry needle: #18
small amount of Dacron batting or other stuffing material
10 wooden beads, each approximately 1 inch long, in yellow
brass ring, 1¼ inches in diameter
inner portion of an embroidery hoop, 6⅜ inches in diameter, painted if desired (we used Testor's Model Paint in copper)
2½ yards grosgrain ribbon, ⅜ inch wide, in yellow

Gauge in Single Crochet: *B and E hooks:* 11 stitches = 2 inches; *G and H hooks:* 9 stitches = 2 inches

The Gingerbread Boys

Body and Head (Make two pieces with each size hook): Starting at bottom with the right leg, ch 2. Then work 3 sc in the 2nd ch from hook, ch 1, and turn. *Next Row:* Inc 1 st at beg of row, work across 3 sts, inc 1 st at end of row. *Next 10 Rows:* Work even. Fasten off. Make another piece in the same manner for the left leg, but do not fasten off. Instead, ch 1 and turn at the end of the 10th row; then start the body. *Next Row:* Work across 5 sts, ch 1, and then attach right leg by working across its top 5 sts, ch 1, and turn. *Next 9 Rows:* Work even on 11 sts, ch 9 at the end of the last row for the right arm, and turn. *Next Row:* Sc in the 2nd ch from hook and in each of the next 7 ch, sc across 11 body sts, ch 9 at the end of the row for the left arm, and turn. *Next Row:* Sc in 2nd ch from hook and in each of next 7 ch, sc to end of row, ch 1, and turn (27 sts). *Next 2 Rows:* Work even and turn at the end of 2nd row. *Next Row:* Sl st across 8 sts, sc to end of row, turn. *Next Row:* Sl st across 11 sts, sc in each of the next 5 sts, ch 1, and turn. Work 1 row on 5 sts and then start the head: Inc 1 st at beg of next row, work across 5 sts, and inc 1 st at end of row. Rep this inc on every row until there are 13 sts; ch 1 and turn at end of the last row. *Next Row:* Skip 1 sc, sc to within last 2 sts, skip 1 st, sc in last st, ch 1, and turn. Rep this row until 3 sts remain. Fasten off. *Finishing:* Attach yarn at bottom of one leg and, with right side of work facing, work 1 row of sc around each piece, increasing sts as necessary so that work lies flat.

Eyes (Make two pieces with each size hook): Using same size hook as was used for piece being trimmed and Color B, ch 5 and join with a sl st to form a ring. Fasten off and sew in position, as shown in the project photograph. Using color A, denote each pupil with a small V st.

Buttons (Make three pieces with each size hook): With Color A and same size hook as used for piece, ch 2, work 5 sc in 2nd ch from hook, fasten off, and sew in position.

Nose: With A, embroider a cross stitch on each piece.

Mouth: With C, embroider four running back stitches.

Assembling: Join each set of two pieces by sewing them together, stuffing them lightly as you sew. Attach double strands of MC to the center top of each head. Using a G hook, ch 60 with each double strand and fasten off. String one bead on the chain attached to the largest of the gingerbread boys, two on the next one smaller in size, three on the next smaller, and four on the smallest. Still using double strands of MC and the G hook, sc around the brass ring, using as many sts as necessary to cover it completely. Next, wrap the portion above the beads on one chain once around the embroidery hoop, make a knot, and, stretching the remainder of the chain taut, sew it to one of the sc sts around the brass ring. Add the other three chains in the same way, spacing them equally around the ring. Finally, make eight small bows with the yellow ribbon and sew one on each side of the neck of each gingerbread boy.

4
Hide 'n Seek Gingerbread Toy

When is a gingerbread man a sandwich? When you crochet gingerbread men in four different sizes, sew snaps on the three largest, and fit all four together in graduated order, one inside another. It's simple to make all four men—you just increase the crochet hook size and the number of strands of yarn, and use the same easy stitch directions for all. If you're making gifts for two children in a family, make the Gingerbread Jamboree for an infant, the Hide 'n Seek Gingerbread Toy for toddlers and young children. Size is fascinating to children, so what could be better than a toy that has four sizes (the smallest is about 6 inches, the largest about 14), is cuddly, and has cookie-characters hidden inside!

Materials:

4 balls (1 ounce each) Spinnerin Frostlon Petite in rust (MC)

small amounts of lightweight yarn in black (A), medium blue (B), red (C), and yellow (D)

4 aluminum crochet hooks: sizes B, G, I, and K

24 snap fasteners, approximately ⅜ inch in diameter

Gauge in Single Crochet: *B hook:* 11 stitches = 2 inches; *G hook:* 9 stitches = 2 inches; *I hook:* 7 stitches = 2 inches, using double strands of yarn; *K hook:* 5 stitches = 2 inches, using triple strands of yarn

The Gingerbread Toy

Following the directions given for the dancing Gingerbread Boy Jamboree (Project 3), make two head-and-body pieces on each of size B, G, I, and K hooks, working to the gauge given above and using the number of strands prescribed for each. Trim one piece only of each set, again following the instructions given in Project 3, this time using the same size hook as that used for each set and, in each instance, using only one strand of yarn and omitting the ribbon bows.

Finishing: After having worked 1 row of sc around each piece, sew together one back and a corresponding trimmed front only halfway around, starting at the bottom center of the left foot and joining along the side of the piece up to the center top of the head. Complete the finishing of each piece by sewing eight snap fasteners evenly spaced along the remaining open portion. To make the bow for the largest of the gingerbread boys, use a G hook and Color D to make a chain approximately 10 inches long, tie it into a bow, and sew it to his front at the neck.

5
Terrance, the Turtle

Terrance will become fast friends with children of any age—young children can sit on his back in the TV room or cuddle up with him at nap time. If you wish, you can insert a zipper around the edge of his shell and Terrance can become a storage bag; older children can stow their pajamas and robe, mothers and infants will have a cheerful diaper storage bag in the nursery. The diameter of Terrance's shell is about 13 inches. He's worked in triple-strand single crochet with detail stitching, and he takes less than eight hours to make.

Materials:

4 balls (4 ounces each) Bernat Berella "4" Knitting Worsted: 2 balls each in sun gold (A) and Shannon green (B) and small amounts of brown (C) and natural (D)

aluminum crochet hook: size K

tapestry needle: #18

Dacron batting or other stuffing material and cardboard disk, approximately 13 inches in diameter, for pillow; or 20-inch zipper for storage bag

Gauge in Single Crochet: 5 stitches = 2 inches, using double strands of yarn

The Turtle

Top Shell: With double strands of A, ch 2. Then work 6 sc in the 2nd ch from hook. *Next Rnd:* Work 2 sc in each sc around (12 sc). Add a marker to denote start of next and all following rnds. *Next Rnd:* *Work 1 sc in the 1st sc, 2 sc in the next sc, rep from * around (18 sc). *Next Rnd:* *Work 1 sc in each of the next 2 sc, 2 sc in the next sc, rep from * around (24 sc). Continue in this manner to inc 6 sts evenly spaced on each rnd, allowing on each rnd 1 st more between each point of increase until there are 114 sc in all. Work even on 114 sts for 4 rnds and then work a picot edging as follows: Sc in the 1st sc, *ch 3, sl st in the 3rd ch from hook, sc in the next sc, rep from * around. Join with a sl st and fasten off.

Bottom Shell: With double strands of B, work as for the top shell until there are 114 sts; join with a sl st and fasten off.

Head: With double strands of B, work as for the shells until there are 30 sc. Work 5 rnds even. *Next Rnd:* Dec 1 st in every other st around (20 sc). Work 3 rnds even. *Next Rnd:* Dec 1 st in every other st around and in the st next to the last (13 sc). Work 5 rnds even; then join with a sl st and fasten off.

Eyes (Make two pieces): With double strands of C, ch 2, work 6 sc in the 2nd ch from hook, join with a sl st, and fasten off. With a single strand of D, *work 2 sc in the 1st sc, 3 sc in the next, rep from * twice, join with a sl st, and fasten off.

Feet (Make four pieces): With double strands of B, ch 11. Work even in sc on 10 sts for 4 rows; then fasten off. Fold each piece in half lengthwise, right sides out, and sew the edges together. Then make four picot-edged toes along one short end of each foot, making the picots in the same manner as those around the top shell.

Tail: With double strands of B, ch 9; then work in sl st across 8 sts and fasten off.

Hat: With double strands of D, make a circle as for the top and bottom shells until there are 18 sc; join with a sl st. Continuing around and joining the end of each rnd with a sl st, work as follows: *Next Rnd:* Ch 1 and, continuing to add 6 sts to make a circle, work through the back lps only of the sts (24 sts). *Next 2 Rnds:* Continuing to inc 6 sts on each rnd, ch 1 and work through both lps (36 sts). *Next Rnd:* Ch 1 and work 2 sc in each sc around. *Next Rnd:* Work even in sc. *Next Rnd:* Sl st around and fasten off.

Trimming: Using the tapestry needle and double strands of A, embroider running chain-stitch markings on the top shell at the following places (see photograph): one length along the full length of each of the six points of increase, one circle around the center stitches of the shell, a second circle 2 inches out from that one, and a third one 2½ inches out from the second one.

With a single strand of C, embroider markings on the bottom shell as follows (see Diagram): Starting with the circular chain trim, embroider a first ring around the center 12 sts of the shell, a second and third one each 1¾ inches out from the one just inside it, and a fourth one 2 inches out from the third one. When the four rounds have been completed, work six lengths of running chain sts, placing one over each point of increase between the first and second circles; a second group of six lengths, placing each of these lengths between the second and third circles and midway between the lengths in the first and second circles; and a third group between the third and fourth circles, again placing each length midway between those on the group above.

Finishing: If the turtle is to be used as a pillow, lay the cardboard disk on the wrong side of the bottom shell and fit the picot edging of the top shell over the bottom. Sew the two pieces together halfway around, stuff them firmly, and sew around the remaining portion. If the turtle is to be used as a diaper bag, omit the cardboard and the stuffing and sew the two pieces together, leaving a 20-inch opening for a zipper; then insert the zipper. When the top and bottom pieces have been joined in the desired manner, stuff the head firmly and sew it to the finished body directly opposite to the center of the zipper if a zipper is being used. Secure it firmly into position with a few tacking stitches. Then sew the eyes to either side of the head. Complete the head by embroidering two nostrils and a large, smiling mouth, as shown in the project photograph, using double strands of C, the tapestry needle, and a running stitch. Stuff the crown of the hat lightly, make a chain of 20 sts with color C, and slide it over the crown of the hat for a hatband. Then sew the hat onto the head. Sew the tail to the outer edge of the bottom shell directly opposite to the center of the neck. Position the two hind feet so that their centers are about 6½ inches from the tail and sew them in place; attach the front feet so that their centers are about 7 inches from the centers of the hind feet. All should be attached to the outer edge of the bottom shell.

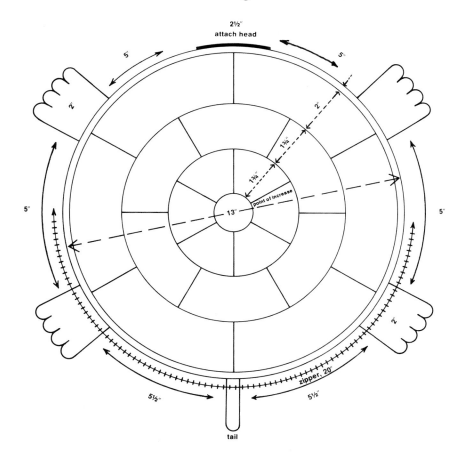

25

6
Tree of Life Sampler

This delightful tree is a flowery keepsake that the newborn and his or her parents will cherish for years to come. Worked in crewel embroidery, this 15- by 24-inch sampler is done with the simple satin, outline, lazy daisy, and stem stitches, with French knots for the perky flower centers. The design can be adopted to any size family by merely adding or subtracting branches. And since the design is a rambling one, you can embroider it in advance—in very little time—and then add the newborn's name and birthdate just before gift-giving time. Instructions for working the stitches, as well as for enlarging and transferring the pattern, are given in Chapter 7.

Materials:

7 skeins (40 yards each) Columbia-Minerva Lady Handicraft Needlepoint
    Yarn: 1 skein each in chestnut, avocado, lettuce green, citron yellow,
    royal wine, pink azalea, and pumpkin
⅝ yard even-weave fabric (such as linen or Indianhead), 36 inches wide, in
    off-white
crewel needle: #4
embroidery hoop, 6⅜ inches in diameter
tracing paper
dressmaker's tracing paper

The Tree of Life

Trace the design and then enlarge it to measure 15 by 24 inches or larger
if desired. Using dressmaker's tracing paper, transfer the design to the cloth
to be embroidered, leaving 3 inches free on each of the four sides of the fabric for trimming and hemming. Then embroider the piece as indicated, adding or eliminating branches and leaves as necessary to accommodate the
number of names to be inscribed. Work all names and dates of birth in the
outline stitch, following the letters and numerals depicted in the alphabet
chart given on page 8.

Finishing: Block the finished piece, turn the unworked edges on each of the
four sides to the wrong side of the work, stitch them into place, and then
mount or frame the piece as desired.

COLOR KEY

1 =*chestnut*
2 =*avocado*
3 =*lettuce green*
4 =*citron yellow*
5 =*royal wine*
6 =*pink azalea*
7 =*pumpkin*

STITCH KEY

CH =*chain stitch*
F =*French knot*
LF =*leaf stitch*
O =*outline stitch*
S =*satin stitch*
ST =*straight stitch*

each square = 1 inch

7
Bluebird Ballet

Four crocheted bluebirds bob merrily from real bird-cage perches to delight any infant or toddler. When suspended over baby's crib, this mobile will also serve as a bright, swaying target for baby to watch while he is developing the ability to focus his eyes. The finished birds on this dancing mobile range from about 5 to 7 inches in size; their features—beaks, eyes, top knot, tail feathers, and wings—are quickly added by crochet or embroidery, adding to the whimsy of these creatures. Since you will need just a little more than two ounces of yarn to make this project, you might use up some of your leftover yarn by crocheting each bird in a different color. This mobile can be ready to please in just about four hours, from start to finish.

Materials:

2 balls (1 ounce each) baby yarn in medium blue (MC)

small amounts knitting worsted in off-white (A), yellow (B), and rust (C)

4 aluminum crochet hooks: sizes E, G, I, and J

small amount of Dacron batting or other stuffing material

tapestry needle: #18

brass ring, 1¼ inches in diameter

2 wooden bird-cage perches, each 8 inches long, painted if desired (we used Testor's Model Paint in copper)

Gauge in Single Crochet: *E hook:* 11 stitches = 2 inches; *G hook:* 5 stitches = 1 inch; *I and J hooks:* 9 stitches = 2 inches

The Birds

Body and Head (Make two pieces with each size hook): With MC, ch 7 and work 6 sc across the row. *Row 2:* Work 3 sc in the 1st st, 1 sc in each of the next 4 sts, and 3 sc in the last st (10 sts). *Row 3:* Work even. *Row 4:* Rep Row 2 (14 sts). *Row 5:* Work even. *Row 6:* Rep Row 2 (18 sts). *Row 7:* Work even; then ch 5 for the tail. *Row 8:* Sc in the 2nd ch from hook and in each of the next 3 ch. Then sc across the rest of the row (22 sts). *Row 9:* Inc 1 st at beg and end of row (24 sts). *Row 10:* Work even. *Row 11:* Inc 1 st at beg and end of row (26 sts). *Row 12:* Work even. *Row 13:* Inc 1 st at beg of row, work in sc across the next 2 sts, sl st in each of the next 5 sts, work in sc across the next 5 sts, sl st in each of the next 4 sts, sc to within the last st, and inc 1 st in the last st (28 sts). *Row 14:* Sc across 10 sts. *Row 15:* Dec 1 st at beg of row; work in sc across the remaining 8 sts. *Row 16:* Work in sc to within the last 2 sts; then dec 1 st. Rep Row 16 until 3 sts remain. Fasten off. *Finishing:* Work 1 rnd of sc around each piece, keeping the work flat and rounding out the head portion. Sew each set of two pieces together with an overcast st, right sides out, stuffing them as you go.

Wings (Make two pieces with each size hook): Using MC and the same size hook as for the bird, ch 2 and work 3 sc in the 2nd ch from hook. *Row 2:* Work even. *Row 3:* Inc 1 st at beg and end of row. *Row 4:* Work even. *Rows 5 and 6:* Rep Rows 3 and 4. *Rows 7 and 8:* Dec 1 st at beg and end of the row. *Rows 9 and 10:* Dec 1 st at beg of row only; then finish the wing by working 1 rnd of sc around the entire piece. With Color C, embroider 5 outline stitches across each wing as shown in the project photograph; then sew the wings to the body of the bird.

Beak: With Color B and an E hook, ch 2 and then work 2 sc in the 2nd ch from hook. *Next Row:* Work 2 sc in each sc. *Next Row:* Work even. Fasten off and sew the beak in position, as shown in the project photograph.

Feet (Make two pieces with each size hook): With Color B and size E hook, ch 4. Work even on 3 sc for 3 rows. *Next Row:* *Ch 4, sl st in the 1st sc, rep from * twice more, and fasten off. Sew the feet in position, as shown in the project photograph.

Eyes (Make two pieces with each size hook): With Color A and size G hook, ch 3. Work 8 sc in the 2nd ch from hook and fasten off. Embroider a Color C French knot in the center of each eye and then sew the eyes in place, as shown in the project photograph.

Tail and Head Feathers: Using Color C, cut six strands of yarn, each measuring 3 inches. Knot two strands at the top of the head and two at the tip of the tail. Knot the remaining two strands to the top of the head so that they will fall in the opposite direction from the head feathers already knotted, to make bangs.

Assembling: Using Color A and a G hook, work as many sc as necessary around the brass ring to cover it completely (approximately 36 sc). Fasten off and reattach the yarn to any sc on the ring. Ch 50, wrap the chain once around the center of one of the wooden perches, and knot it tightly in place. Continuing on, ch 30 more sts, fasten off, and attach this length of chain in the same manner to the second of the perches. Attach the birds to the perches in the following manner: Make four separate chains, one 6 inches long for the largest bird, one 7 inches long for the next largest, an 8-inch chain for the third largest, and a 9-inch chain for the smallest. For balance, hang the two smaller birds from the lower perch; the smallest bird should hang under the largest one and the next smallest under the second largest. Slip one end of one chain into one of the grooves of the perch and knot it around the stick; then draw the other end under a few stitches across the back of the bird and knot it to the remainder of the chain, as shown in the project photograph, approximately 1½ inches above the back of the bird. Repeat this procedure until all four birds are attached.

8
The Delicate Air: A Soft and Simple Child's Shawl

Any little one will feel warm and secure when wrapped from head to toe in this lacy shawl or snuggled underneath it in his carriage. When the shawl's not in use, lay it over the back of a wooden rocking chair to brighten a room a bit—or to be ready to offer baby some extra warmth during a rocking session. To make this light and airy coverlet, which measures about 32 by 36 inches, strips of hairpin lace were alternated with strips of crochet in varying widths. Two simple crochet stitches and a large hook create the shell-like pattern, and uncut fringe delicately borders the whole piece.

Materials:
4 balls (3½ ounces each) Unger's Roly-Poly in yellow #901
adjustable hairpin-lace loom
aluminum crochet hook: size G (for hairpin lace)
wood crochet hook: #15 (for crochet work)
tapestry needle: #18

Crochet Pattern Stitch: *Row 1:* (1 sc, 1 dc) in 2nd ch from hook, *skip 1 ch, (1 sc, 1 dc) in the next ch, rep from * across, and end 1 sc in the last ch, ch 1, turn. *Row 2:* *(1 sc, 1 dc) in the next sc, skip 1 dc, rep from * across, and end 1 sc in the last sc, ch 1, and turn. Rep Row 2 for pattern.

Gauge in Crochet Pattern Stitch: 5 stitches = 2 inches

The Shawl

Hairpin-Lace Strips: With the loom adjusted to 2 inches, make six strips, keeping the spine in the center and making 86 lps on each side. Readjust the loom to 4 inches and make 1 strip of 516 lps on each side for the border, this time keeping the spine ¼ inch in from the right-side edge. Finish each of the 2-inch strips by working 1 row of sc along each long edge, using the #15 hook and twisting each lp as you work. Finish the 4-inch strip in the same manner, this time working only the edge along the lps closest to the spine and working 2 lps together as you go.

Crochet Strips: Make six 36-inch-long strips, two on 9 sts to measure about 3¾ inches wide, two on 5 sts to measure 2 inches wide, and two on 3 sts to measure approximately 1¼ inches wide.

Finishing: With right side of work facing, alternate the crochet strips with the 2-inch hairpin-lace strips, placing the crocheted strips in the following order: *one 3¾-inch strip, one 2-inch strip, one 1¼-inch strip, *then two 2-inch hairpin-lace strips together; rep from between *'s, reversing the order and ending with one 3¾-inch crochet strip. Using the same yarn, sew all strips together with an overcast stitch. Work one row of sc along the entire outer edge, working 3 sc in each corner as you go. Sew the 4-inch strip of hairpin-lace around the edge, joining 59 sc sts along each short end of the piece and 70 along each long edge and sewing together the spines of the border hairpin-lace strips as they meet in each of the four corners.

9
A Warm and Furry Pram Robe

When Jack Frost's in town, this lined pram robe will keep baby cozy, although the piece could just as easily be used as a textury, toe-wriggling rug for the nursery, as we pictured it. Its clean, two-color geometric pattern would also make it work well as a wall hanging, particularly in any expansive contemporary setting. If you would prefer to give this piece a softer, more subtle look, work it up in a tone-on-tone combination—try two different hues of muted green or a pale lemon with sunniest yellow or a dusty pink with mauve. The loopy diamond shapes of the rug are quickly worked with a latchet hook on a rug-canvas backing; the flat contrast strips are simply single crocheted and then hand-sewn to the canvas. If you'd like to make this piece larger— it measures about 2½ by 3 feet—simply add more repeats of the diamond design.

Materials:

14 packs (1.9 ounces each) Brunswick Pre-Cut Rug Wool in ecru
4 skeins (4 ounces each) Brunswick Brunsana (3-ply knitting worsted weight) in powder blue
rug canvas, 7 spaces to 2 inches, 28 x 36 inches
masking tape
latchet hook
aluminum crochet hook: size K
1 yard lining fabric, 36 inches wide, in powder blue

Gauge in Single Crochet: 7 stitches = 2 inches, using double strands of yarn

The Robe

Bind all four edges of the rug canvas with masking tape. Mark off a 2½-inch-wide border around all edges of the rug canvas and turn the canvas so that one of the shorter dimensions is facing you. Starting in the lower right-hand corner of the piece, begin to hook with the rug yarn, following the design chart. Fill each triangle and each center diamond, working each row from right to left. Repeat the design a total of 12 times and then fill in the unworked areas with strips of single crochet, working each strip on 4 sts with double strands of the powder blue yarn. Start by making two 6-inch strips, two 17-inch strips, two 26-inch strips, and one 32-inch strip. Place these strips as they fit in the diagonal unworked spaces, working either from the upper left-hand corner to the lower right-hand corner or from the upper right-hand corner to the lower left; pin them in place. Now make twenty-four strips on the same number of stitches, each to measure 3½ inches, and pin them in place between the diagonal strips. Then make two 2½-inch strips for the top and bottom borders and two 32½-inch strips for the left and right borders. Pin these in place. Now, tucking all extended pieces under adjacent pieces, stitch them in place so that they lie flat, sewing them with a needle and matching thread.

Finishing: Turn 1 inch of the unworked canvas to the wrong side of the work and hem into place. Cut lining to fit the finished piece, turn the edges under to lie against the canvas, and overcast it to the top.

COLOR KEY

 =ecru   =powder blue

36

10
Her Special Outfit for Special Events

A feathery hairpin-lace vest slips gracefully over a knitted pullover, to be worn with anything from denims to a long patchwork skirt. Either piece can, of course, be worn separately, with the pullover making a real contribution to a basic wardrobe and the vest standing ready to offer a dress-up touch to almost any other outfit. The pullover has a folded-down turtleneck, set-in sleeves, and hemmed edges (no ribbing!). The vest is worked on an adjustable hairpin-lace loom in strips, which are then finished in easy crochet stitches and joined with an overcast stitch. A simple fringe decorates the bottom edge. The directions for this project are given for a size 4; changes for sizes 6, 8, 10, and 12 follow in parentheses. You can make both pieces for your favorite girl over a weekend.

Above, from left to right: *Her Special Outfit for Special Events, p. 37; A Sweater Just Like Dad's, p. 41.* Left: *All in the Family: Caps and Scarves, p. 43.*

Materials:
5 (6,6,8,9) balls (1.4 ounces each) Unger Cruise: 3 (4,4,5,6) balls #44 (A)
for the slipover and 2 (2,2,3,3) balls #59 (B) for the vest
2 pairs straight knitting needles: #4 and #5
aluminum crochet hook: size D
adjustable hairpin-lace loom

Gauge in Stockinette Stitch: 6 stitches = 1 inch; 8 rows = 1 inch

The Pullover

Back: With #4 needles, cast on 68 (72,78,84,90) sts. Work in stockinette st for 1 inch, ending on the wrong side of the work. Then p 1 row on the right side of the work for the hemline. Continuing in stockinette st, work 1 inch more. Change to #5 needles and work even until piece measures 9 (10,11,11½,12) inches above the hemline. *Shape Armholes:* Bind off 3 (3,3,4,4) sts at beg of each of the next 2 rows; then dec 1 st at beg and end of every other row 2 (2,3,3,3) times. Work even now on 58 (62,66,70,76) sts until piece measures 4½ (5,5½,6,6½) inches above the start of the armhole shaping. *Shape Shoulders:* Bind off 8 (9,10,11,12) sts at beg of each of the next 4 rows; then bind off loosely the remaining 26 (26,26,26,28) sts for back of neck.

Front: Work as for back until piece measures 2(2½,3,3½,4) inches above the start of the armhole shaping. *Shape Neck:* Work across 19 (21,23,25,27) sts, bind off center 20 (20,20,20,22) sts, then join another ball of yarn, and work across remaining 19 (21,23,25,27) sts. Working on both sides at once now, dec 1 st at each neck edge every other row 3 times; then work even on 16 (18,20,22,24) sts of each side until piece measures same as back to the shoulders. Shape shoulders as for back.

Sleeves: With #4 needles, cast on 30 (34,36,38,40) sts for each sleeve. Work in stockinette st for 1 inch, ending on the wrong side of the work; then p 1 row on the right side of the work for the hemline. Continuing in stockinette st, work even for 1 inch more. Change to #5 needles and work even for ¾ inch. Then inc 1 st at beg and end of next row and rep this inc every ¾ inch until there are 54 (58,60,66,70) sts. Work even now until piece measures 10½ (11½,12½,13½,15) inches above the hemline. *Shape Caps:* Bind off 3 (3,3,4,4) sts at beg of each of the next 2 rows and then dec 1 st at beg and end of every other row for 2 (2,2½,3,3½) inches. Bind off 3 sts at beg of each of the next 6 rows; then bind off the remaining sts.

Finishing: Sew sleeve seams, side seams, and one shoulder seam. Sew in sleeves.

Collar: With right side of work facing, pick up and knit 78 (82,84,86,90) sts around the neck edge. Continue in pat st as now established for 2 (2,2½,2½,3) inches, ending on the wrong side of the work. Then p 1 row on the right side of the work and work in reverse stockinette st for 2 (2,2½,2½,3) inches more. Bind off loosely and sew remaining shoulder and collar seam. Then work 3 rnds of sc around the bound-off collar edge and 1 rnd around the top turnover edge, working this last rnd from left to right instead of right to left. Turn under the sleeve and bottom hems at hemlines and sew into place.

The Vest

Make eight hairpin-lace strips, two with the loom adjusted to 3 (3¼,4,4,4)

inches for 26 (28,30,32,34) lps, four on a 2½ (2½,3,3,4)-inch loom for 26 (28,30,32,34) lps, and two more on a 1½-inch loom for 100 (104,108,112,116) lps. Work off the lps on each side of each strip in the following manner: *1 sc through the next 2 lps together, twisting them as you go, ch 2, rep from * across the entire strip, ch 1, and turn at the end of the row. On the next row, work 1 sc in each sc and 2 sc in each ch-2 space. (For size 10 only, work 1 additional row of sc on each side of the two 4-inch strips, working 1 sc in each sc along the row; for size 12 only, work 2 additional rows of sc on each side of the two 4-inch strips being used as the center strips.) When completed, arrange the strips as follows: one 3 (3¼,4,4,4)-inch strip at the center front and one at the center back; one 1-inch strip along each side of the center front, over the shoulders, and along each side of the center back (these strips serve as straps; to determine how much strap to allow for the shoulders, match the short edges with the bottoms of the center front and back pieces); and one 2½ (2½,3,3,4)-inch strip along each long unattached edge of the strap strips, to serve as side pieces. Join the strips by sewing them together with an overcast st.

Finishing: *Bottom edge:* Attach yarn at one side edge and then work 2 sc in the sc joining, ch 6 (6,7,7,8) over half of the 2½ (2½,3,3,4)-inch lace strip on the front edge, work 1 sc in the spine, ch 6 (6,7,7,8) over the other half of the strip; work 4 sc in the next joining, ch 2 over half of the 1½-inch strip, work 1 sc in the spine, ch 2 over the other half of that strip; work 4 sc in the next joining, ch 9 (9,10,10,11) over half of the 3 (3¼,4,4,4)-inch strip, work 1 sc in the spine, ch 9 (9,10,10,11) over the other half of that strip, work 4 sc in the next joining, work over the second 1½-inch strip as on the first and over the last front 2½ (2½,3,3,4)-inch strip as the first; then work across the back edge to correspond with the front. On the next round, work 1 sc in each sc and each ch around. On the last round, work 1 sc in each sc. Fasten off. *Front neck edge:* Attach yarn in joining at one side of the center front strip, work 2 sc in that joining, ch 9 (9,10,10,11) over half the 3 (3¼,4,4,4)-inch strip, work 1 sc in the spine, ch 9 (9,10,10,11) over the other half of that strip, and work 2 sc in the next joining. Then ch 1, turn, and work 1 sc in each sc and in each ch across that row. Work the back neck edging in the same manner. Then work 1 rnd of sc around the entire neck opening, including the inner strap edges. *Armhole edge:* Attach yarn at the side joining of one armhole and work 2 sc in that joining. Then ch 6 (6,7,7,8) over half of the 2½ (2½,3,3,4)-inch strip, work 1 sc in the spine, ch 6 (6,7,7,8) over the other half of that strip, and work 2 sc in the next joining. Ch 1, turn, and work 1 sc in each sc and each ch across that row. Complete the armhole by working 1 rnd of sc around the entire opening, including the outer strap edges. Finish the other armhole opening in the same manner. *Fringe:* Slip the vest over the sweater and cut strands of yarn to measure ¾ inch longer than twice the length of the space between the bottom of the vest and the bottom of the slipover. Knot two strands of yarn in every other stitch around.

11
A Sweater Just Like Dad's

Knitted bands edge the fronts and neck of this knitted V-neck cardigan, made especially in a denim-look yarn to appeal to the roughest, readiest boy on the block. Set-in sleeves with ribbed cuffs and two buttons placed side by side at the lower edge are the other features of this sweater "exactly like Dad's." Although the cardigan is quite substantial, it's possible to make it in just about eight hours. The directions are written for a size 4; changes for sizes 6, 8, 10, and 12 are given in parentheses.

Materials:

2 (2,2,3,3) skeins (4 ounces each) Columbia-Minerva Nantuk Denim 4-ply yarn in blue

2 pairs straight knitting needles: #5 and #8

2 buttons, each ¾ inch in diameter

Pattern Stitch: *Row 1 (right side):* Purl; *Row 2:* Knit. Repeat these 2 rows for pattern.

Gauge in Pattern Stitch: 9 stitches = 2 inches

The Sweater

Back: With #5 needles, cast on 52 (54,58,64,68) sts. Work in k 1, p 1 ribbing for 1½ (1¾,2,2¼,2½) inches. Change to #8 needles and pat st and work even until piece measures 9 (10,11,11½,12) inches. *Shape Armholes:* Bind off 2 (2,3,3,3) sts at beg of each of the next 2 rows; then dec 1 st at beg and end of every other row 2 (2,2,3,3) times. Work even now on 44 (46,48,52,56) sts until piece measures 4½ (5,5½,6,6½) inches above the start of the armhole shaping. *Shape Shoulders:* Bind off 7 (7,8,8,9) sts at beg of each of the next 2 rows and 6 (7,7,8,8) sts at beg of each of the next 2 rows. Bind off loosely remaining 18 (18,18,20,22) sts for back of neck.

Right Front: With #5 needles, cast on 36 (38,40,42,44) sts. Work in k 1, p 1 ribbing for 1½ (1¾,2,2¼,2½) inches. *Next Row:* To make front edge, work in ribbing across 4 sts and slip these sts on a stitch holder to be worked later; purl across the remaining 32 (34,36,38,40) sts. Working in pat st now, work even for 1 inch; then dec 1 st at front edge and repeat this dec every ¾ (¾,¾,1,1) inch until piece measures same as back to underarm, ending at side edge. *Shape Armhole:* Bind off 2 (2,3,3,3) sts at beg of next row; then dec 1 st at same edge every other row 2 (2,2,3,3) times. Work even at side edge now and continue to dec 1 st at front edge every ¾ (¾,¾,1,1) inch until 13 (14,15,16,17) sts remain. Work even until piece measures same as back to shoulder, ending at the side edge. *Shape Shoulder:* Bind off 7 (7,8,8,9) sts once and 6 (7,7,8,8) sts once. Fasten off.

Left Front: Work to correspond to right front, reversing all shaping and working in two buttonholes (instructions follow) on the bottom ribbing after ¾ (¾,1,1,1½) inches have been worked, the first one on the fourth and fifth sts in from the front edge and the second one after 3 inches of ribbing have been worked. *To Make Buttonholes:* Bind off 2 sts. On the next row, cast on 2 sts over those bound off on the previous row.

Sleeves: With #5 needles, cast on 23 (25,27,29,31) sts for each sleeve. Work in k 1, p 1 ribbing for 1¾ (1¾,2,2,2½) inches. Change to #8 needles and pat st and work even for ¾ inch. At beg and end of next row, inc 1 st; rep this increase every ¾ inch until there are 41 (43,45,49,53) sts. Work even now until piece measures 10½ (11½,12½,13½,15) inches in all. *Shape Caps:* Bind off 2 (2,3,3,3) sts at beg of each of the next 2 rows. Then dec 1 st at beg and end of every other row for 2 (2,2½,3,3½) inches. Bind off 2 sts at beg of each of the next 6 rows; then bind off remaining sts.

Front Bands: Sl 4 sts from right front stitch holder onto #5 needles and work in k 1, p 1 ribbing until piece measures up front and around neck to center back. Bind off. Work left front band in same manner.

Finishing: Sew side and sleeve seams. Sew in sleeves. Sew front bands in place and seam the ends together at the center back. Sew on buttons.

12
All in the Family: Caps and Scarves

Contrasting stripes are the eye-catchers on these matched crocheted cap-and-scarf sets for the family. Everyone will know that Mom has seniority with three stripes on her scarf, that the "older one" has grown up to a two-stripe status, and that the toddler is happy just looking at his bright single one. On the hats, the stripes march gaily right up to the lightly stuffed pom-poms; the folded-up cuffs of the hats will keep ears extra warm. The toddler's hat measures about 17 inches around the bottom; the child's about 19 inches; the woman's about 21 inches —all stretch a bit to fit the head snugly. The scarves measure about 34 inches, 36 inches, and 60 inches, not counting the fringe. You can crochet the three sets in less than a weekend.

Materials:
5 (5,6) skeins (4 ounces each) Coats & Clark's Red Heart Fabulend Knitting
Worsted: 1 (1,2) skein in eggshell (MC) and 1 skein each in skipper blue
(A), devil red (B), emerald green (C), and lemon (D) for each size *or* 3
skeins MC and 1 skein each of A, B, C, and D for all three sets
aluminum crochet hook: size J
small amount of Dacron batting or other stuffing material

Pattern Stitch: *Row 1:* 1 sc in 2nd ch from hook, *1 dc in next ch, 1 sc in
next ch, rep from * across and end 1 sc in last ch, ch 2, turn; *Row 2:* *1
dc in next sc, 1 sc in next dc, rep from * across and end 1 dc in last
sc, ch 1, turn; *Row 3:* *1 sc in next dc, 1 dc in next sc, rep from * across
and end 1 sc in last dc, ch 2, turn. Repeat rows 2 and 3 for pattern.

Gauge in Pattern Stitch: 3 stitches = 1 inch; 10 rows = 3 inches

The Scarves

With MC, ch 16 (20,22). Work in pat st on 15 (19,21) sts for 4 rows. Then work
a sc striped pat using 2 rows A, 2 rows B, 2 rows C, 2 rows D, and 2 rows
A. Return to MC pat now and work for 2 rows. Repeat the striped pat with 2
rows MC pat between 0 (1,2) times. Now, work even in MC pat until piece
measures 34 (36,60) inches in all, or desired length. Fasten off. To make the
fringe, cut strands of MC yarn to measure 3 (5,7) inches long and knot two
strands in each st along both short ends of the scarf.

The Caps

With MC, ch 44 (48,52). Work in pat st on 43 (47,51) sts for 4 (6,8) inches,
decreasing 1 (0,3) sts evenly spaced on last row. On the medium-size cap,
inc 1 st on last row. Change now to the sc striped pat. Repeat a color sequence of A, B, C, and D (omitting the 9th and 10th Color A rows used on
the scarves) and, *at the same time,* when 4 (4,8) rows of striped pat have
been completed, work as follows: *Next Row:* *Work across 5 (6,6) sts, work
the next 2 sts tog, rep from * across row. Work even on 36 (42,42) sts for 1
row. *Next Row:* Work across 4 (5,5) sts, work next 2 sts tog, rep from * across
row. Work even on 30 (36,36) sts for 1 row. Continue now to dec 6 sts on
every other row, allowing 1 st less between each point of decrease, until 6
sts remain. Fasten off, leaving a thread approximately 6 inches long; then
draw thread tightly through the remaining 6 sts.

Finishing: Sew back seam, using the same color yarn to sew each stripe as
that with which it was crocheted. Stuff top 1 (1½,2) inch of cap firmly and secure stuffing in place on the wrong side of the work by sewing a small MC
circle over it. To make the circle: Ch 6, join with a sl st to form a ring, and
then work 12 sc in the center of the ring. Join with a sl st and fasten off.

44

2

The Little Pleasures Shop for Her

13
The Hooded Scarf

Not only chic and warm, this hooded scarf is also convenient; you don't have to fumble with both a hat and a scarf or worry about losing your paraphernalia as you come and go. A flattering cuff at the front of the hood frames your face, and a single contrasting stripe crosses each end of the scarf. Loopy yarn gives a beautiful texture to the two-toned project, which is easy to make because the pieces are all single crocheted and then simply stitched together. In fact, you can make this piece in just five hours.

The Hooded Scarf, p. 46.

Materials:
8 skeins (1 ounce each) Spinnerin Genie, 4 skeins in deep red #6250 (A) and
    4 skeins in misty green #6214 (B)
aluminum crochet hook: size K

Gauge in Single Crochet: 5 stitches = 2 inches

The Hooded Scarf

The Scarf (Make two pieces, one in Color A with a Color B stripe and the other in B with an A stripe): Ch 21, work on 20 sc for 6 inches, and then dec 1 st at each end of the row; rep this dec every 4 inches twice more. *At the same time,* when the piece measures 6 inches, work a 2-inch-wide stripe in the contrasting color. Returning to the starting color, work 22 inches more. Fasten off.

The Hood (Make two pieces, one in Color A and one in Color B): Ch 29 and work on 28 sc for 11 inches. Fasten off.

Finishing: Join the two hood pieces by sewing them together along the narrower ends for the top of the hood and the wider ends for the back. Turn back 3 inches around the hood to make a front cuff and tack this in place. Sew together the narrow ends of the two scarf pieces and join this seam to the back seam of the hood. Then sew the side edges of the scarf to the bottom edges of the hood (with the turned-back cuff at the front).

14
For Fun at the Beach

You'll make a splash in any pool in this lovely crocheted bikini. It's simple to make—you can work it up the day before the beach party—but more important, it's both machine washable and dryable. The pattern is elegant in its simplicity and especially stunning with its detail of circular brass rings. Directions are written for the small size (8–10). Changes for the medium size (12–14) are provided in parentheses.

For Fun at the Beach, p. 49.

Materials:

4 (5) balls (1.4 ounces each) Unger Cruise in white
steel crochet hook: #10
2 packages (2 yards each) elastic, ⅜ inch wide
3 brass rings, 1 inch in diameter
fabric for lining (optional)

Gauge in Single Crochet: 8 stitches = 1 inch; 8 rows = 1 inch

The Bottom

Back: Working in sc throughout and starting at the crotch, ch 29. Work even on 28 sts for 4 rows. Inc 1 st at beg and end of the next row and on each of the next 39 rows (108 sts). Ch 5 (13) at the end of the last row. Now, work in sc across the 4 (12) ch and the 108 sc; ch 5 (13) at the end of the row. Then work in sc across the 4 (12) ch and across the remaining 112 (120) sts on the row (116 [132] sts). Work even on these sts for 1 (2) inch and fasten off.

Front: Again starting at the crotch, ch 29 and work even in sc on 28 sts for 4 rows. Dec 1 st now at beg and end of the next row; rep this dec every other row 3 times more (20 sts). Work even until piece measures 5 inches in all. Then inc 1 st at beg and end of the next row and on each of the next 23 rows (68 sts). Ch 25 (33) at the end of the last row. Work in sc across the 24 (32) ch and the remaining 68 sts on the row. Ch 25 (33) at the end of the last row. *Next Row:* Work in sc across the 24 (32) ch and across the remaining 92 (100) sts on the row (116 [132] sts). Work even now on these sts for 1 (2) inch. Fasten off.

Finishing: Sew the crotch seam. To edge the leg openings, have the right side of the work facing. Attach yarn to the top of the front at the point where 25 (33) sts were chained, and work in sc around to the point on the back where 5 (13) sts were chained. Work back and forth on these sts for 6 rows. Work another row of sc on these sts, working through only the back lps of the sts for a turnover hem, and then work 5 more rows of sc in the usual manner. Fasten off. Work the edging along the other leg opening in the same manner. To edge the waistband, work 12 rows of sc for each edging in the same way as the edgings around the leg openings. Cut two pieces of elastic, each 19 (21) inches, for the leg openings and two 13 (14)-inch pieces for the waistband. Turn each edging to the inside, folding it along the hemline and over the elastic cut to fit each piece. Hem these edgings in place, securely stitching down the short ends of the elastic. To add the brass rings to the sides, attach yarn to the top of any of the four short waistband edges, ch 12, draw the chain through a ring, and secure the end of it with a sl st in the same place that the yarn was originally attached. Make another chain in the center of that same short edge and attach it to the ring in the same manner; then make a third one, placing this one at the bottom of the edge. Secure the other side of the ring in the same manner, placing the three chains so that they correspond to those on the other side. Attach the second ring in the same way on the other side of the piece.

The Top

Cups (Make two pieces): Working in sc throughout, ch 52 (60) and work even on 51 (59) sts for one row. Dec 1 st at beg and end of the next row; rep this dec at beg and end of every other row 13 (15) times more and then at beg and end of every row 8 (10) times. When 7 sts remain, fasten off.

Finishing: With right side of work facing and following the instructions for the bikini bottom, make a 12-row edging around the two side edges of each cup, working from one bottom corner up to the point and then down to the opposite bottom corner. Cut two pieces of elastic, each 10 (11) inches, insert these pieces into the middle of the edgings, fold under the edgings at the hemline, and finish them as for the other edgings. To make the bottom edging and back band, hold the two cups upside down and, with right side of the work facing, work in sc across the starting stitches of the left cup, ch 96 (112), then work across the starting sts of the right cup, ch 1, and turn. On the next row, work 1 sc in each sc and in each ch across the row. Continuing on these sts, work 4 more rows of sc, then a turnover row of sc through the back lps of the sts only, and finally another 5 rows in the usual manner. Fasten off. Cut a piece of elastic to measure 25 (27) inches and finish this elasticized turnover hem in the same manner as the others. To connect the cups in the center to the brass ring, work six chains of 12 sts each, attaching each along the short open end of the turned-under edge of the bottom of the piece, and finish them in the same manner as those on the bikini bottom. Finally, finish this part of the bikini by making two single-crochet straps, each on 6 sts for 14 inches, or desired length. When the straps have been completed, work 1 row of sl st around the four sides and sew one short end of each one to the front point of each cup, leaving the other end free for tying.

15
The Carryall

The carryall, made with bulky yarn and heavy rug canvas, is highly styled. Worked in bright, cheerful colors of tangerine, scarlet, and sapphire, it is smartly finished with four wide metal D rings. The inside is fully lined for a neat, professional effect. Take it everywhere; use it as a carryall, a portfolio, or a rather unusual overnight bag.

Materials:

11 skeins (2 ounces each) Columbia-Minerva Nantuk Bulky: 4 skeins in
tangerine, 4 skeins in scarlet, and 3 skeins in sapphire
rug canvas, 7 spaces to 2 inches, 24 × 30 inches
masking tape
4 metal D rings, each 1¾ inches wide
aluminum crochet hook: size K
2 pieces poster paper, each 21 × 27 inches
plastic or other lining material, 24 × 30 inches
blunt-ended embroidery needle with a very large eye
heavy-duty zipper, 20 inches long
small amount of cotton batting, polyfoam, or other stuffing material

Gauge in Single Crochet: 2 stitches = 1 inch

The Carryall

Bind the edges of the canvas with masking tape. Then fold the canvas in half
along the 30-inch dimension. Leaving 4 spaces free at each side edge for
trimming and hemming, start the work at point A. Using double strands of
yarn and the continental stitch throughout and following the color key, work
from A to B once and from A to C four times. When this portion of the work
has been completed, turn the piece to the opposite side and work the remaining unworked portion of the canvas in exactly the same way.

For the crocheted portion of the work, use double strands of sapphire. To
make the short tabs for the handles, first close the small openings on the D
rings with masking tape to prevent the sts from slipping through. Then work
3 sc over the flat side of one ring, ch 1, and turn. Work even on these 3 sts
for 3 inches and fasten off. Repeat this step on the other three rings. Sew two
tabs to each side of the carryall, placing each so that the flat side of the D
ring is about 1 inch down from the top of the canvas and the outer edge of
the tab is about 6 inches in from the side edge of the canvas. To make the
handles, work 3 sc over the curved portion of one of the rings, ch 1, and turn.
Work even on these 3 sts for 3 inches and then inc 1 st in each st across.
Work even now on 6 sts for 9 inches, then dec 1 st in each st across the row,
and work even on 3 sts for 3 inches more. Fasten off and sew this end to the
other ring on the same side of the bag. Make the handle for the other side
of the bag in the same way and add it to the bag.

Finishing: Holding the two sheets of poster paper together, score them
through the center along their 27-inch dimension so that they will fold easily
in half. Then place them over the underside of the finished canvas, remove
the tape from the canvas edges, fold the edges to the underside and place
them under the double sheets of poster paper, and tape or staple the edges
of the poster paper to the canvas. Cut the lining material now so that it is ½
inch larger all around than the canvas. Lay the lining over the poster paper,
turn the ½-inch allowance under, and sew the lining to the four worked edges
of the canvas. Now, fold the lined piece in half, right sides out, and sew the
side edges together with a single strand of sapphire yarn and an overcast
stitch, working the overcast stitch first from one side of the needlepoint piece
toward the center and then from the other side toward the center, as shown
in the diagram. Add the zipper to close the top of the carryall. Then stuff the
6-st-wide portion of each of the two handles and sew their side edges together over the stuffing.

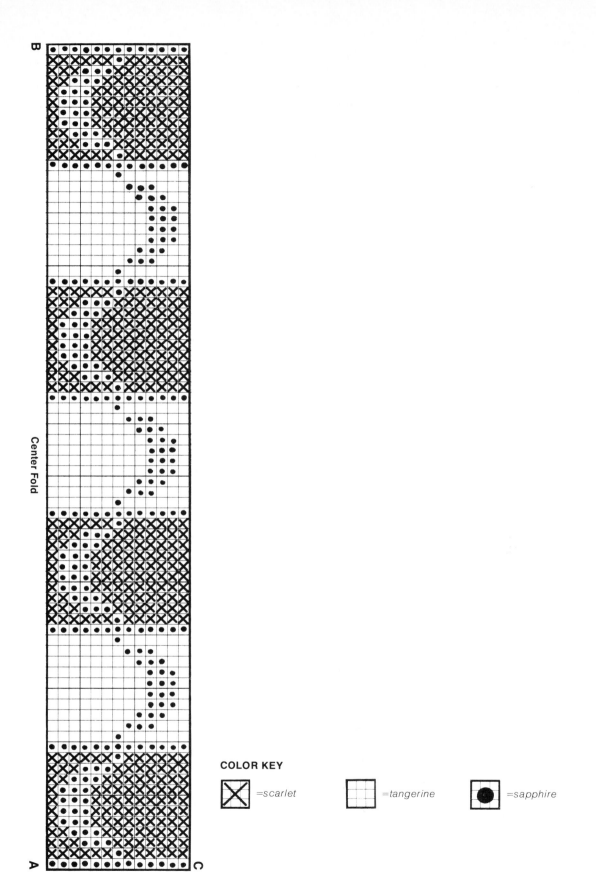

COLOR KEY

=scarlet

=tangerine

=sapphire

55

16
A Festive Shawl

In very little working time, you can transform yarn with a metallic thread into midnight magic. Four strips of fan-shaped hairpin lace are joined into a triangle with basic crochet stitches to make this. A luxurious fringe surrounds the lower edges of the shawl, the longest edge of which measures about 72 inches. When you pack this coverup for out-of-town important occasions, you'll find that it folds up into almost nothing.

Materials:
6 balls (40 grams each) Bernat Dorlaine in fawn mist
adjustable hairpin-lace loom
aluminum crochet hook: size G

The Shawl

Lace: Make five hairpin-lace strips with the loom adjusted to 4 inches, the first strip with 21 lps, the second with 105, the third with 189, the fourth with 273, and the fifth with 357.

Edging: To edge the first strip, *work 3 lps tog with 1 sc, ch 5, rep from * across the row, ch 1, and turn. *Next Row:* Work 1 sc in each sc and 5 sc in each ch-5 lp across. Fasten off. To edge the other side of the strip, work 21 lps tog with 1 sc. Fasten off. To edge the top of the remaining strips, *work 3 lps tog with 1 sc, ch 5, and rep from * 7 times; then work 21 lps tog with 1 sc, ch 5, rep from * 1 (3,5,7) time, and end by *working 3 lps tog with 1 sc, ch 5, and rep from * 6 times; ch 1 and turn. *Next Row:* Work 1 sc in each sc and 5 sc in each ch-5 lp across. Fasten off. To edge the bottom of the strips, work along the opposite edge of the strip. *Work 21 lps tog with 1 sc, ch 5, (work 3 lps tog with 1 sc, ch 5) 7 times, rep from * across the row, and end by working the last 21 lps tog with 1 sc; ch 1 and turn. *Next Row:* Work 1 sc in each sc and 5 sc in each ch-5 lp across. Fasten off.

Finishing: Sew the strips together with an overcast st, sewing the bottom edge of the second strip to the top edge of the first strip, the bottom edge of the third strip to the top edge of the second strip, and so on. Now work around the entire outer edge of the piece in sc, working 1 sc in each sc and 3 sc in the bottom point. In each lace portion where there is no sc, work a ch-10, 1 sc in the spine adjacent to it, and a ch-10 again in the portion of the lace immediately following the spine. Work 1 more rnd of sc, working 1 sc in each sc and ch st around and working 3 sc in the bottom point. Then work a 3rd rnd of sc along the straight top edge only, to shape the front and neck edges, decreasing 1 st in each st on this rnd. For fringe, cut strands of yarn to measure 7 inches long; alternate knotting two of these strands in the 1st st with one in the next, working along the two side edges of the shawl.

17
A Knotted Belt

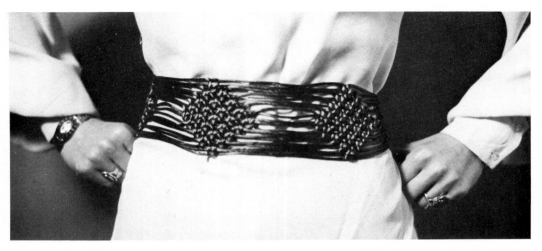

The perfect boutique belt to wear with a classic sweater and skirt or a knitted dress. Picture the glossy deep violet belt shown here cinching the waist of a calf-length white angora pullover. Or pussy willow gray with a sleek black velour jumpsuit. You can macramé this belt in just one afternoon—it calls for only square knots and much of the length is openwork, which helps make the belt wrap softly and gracefully around your waist. The belt is designed for a 24-inch waist—instructions for making it in a smaller or larger size are included in the general project instructions.

From left to right: *The Lace Wraparound, p. 61; A Knotted Belt, p. 58; A Festive Shawl, p. 56.*

Materials:

5 balls (20 yards each) Lily Rattail macramé cord in deep violet for a 24-inch waist

small piece of Styrofoam or lap-size cardboard box for a working surface

The Belt

Cut twenty strands of yarn, each 6 times the diameter of your waist plus an additional 28 inches for 14-inch fringe at each end. Leaving 14 inches free at the starting end, pin the strands individually and close in a straight line across your working surface; then work as follows to make the starting half diamond: *Row 1:* Make five square knots, using four strands for each. *Drop the two outermost strands at either side of the work. *Row 2:* Make four square knots, using four strands for each. Again drop the two outermost strands. *Row 3:* Make three square knots, using four strands for each. Continue in this manner until one square knot has been worked with the center four strands.*

**Working with the center four strands only and leaving 2½ inches of the material unworked (or ¼ inch less for each inch that a waist measurement is smaller and ¼ inch more for each inch that it is larger), continue as follows to make the diamonds: Make one center square knot as the last one on the half diamond. Then pick up the two innermost of the dropped strands on each side and make two square knots, using four strands for each. Continue in this manner, picking up the two innermost of the dropped strands for each new row and working one more four-strand knot on each row until there are five knots across. Work now from between *'s on the half diamond. Repeat from the ** now until three diamonds have been completed. Then work one more half diamond, starting with one square knot and ending with five.

Finishing: Divide the strands at one end into groups of 6, 8, and 6 and use them to make a large square knot at the end; repeat on the other end. Trim all ends evenly and make a slip knot at the end of each one. (Note: If the knots slip a little because of the nature of rattail, secure them with a tacking stitch wherever necessary.)

18
The Lace Wraparound

This alluring scarf can be worn on your head, knotted at your neck, or wrapped around your waist. Sparkly thread and an airy crochet stitch pattern make this gossamer strip just the accessory to pull out for special evenings or to add a little splash to an otherwise-ordinary outfit. There's enough length—just over five feet—to be as dramatic as you like when you wrap this. The center portion of the scarf is ingeniously left unstitched to enable you to wear the scarf on your head.

Materials:
6 skeins (20 grams each) Unger Ariane in pink #9
aluminum crochet hook: size I

Gauge in Single Crochet: 7 stitches = 2 inches; 1 motif = 5 inches in
diameter

The Wraparound

Motifs (Make fourteen): Ch 4 and join with a sl st to form a ring. *Rnd 1:* Ch 3 (counts as 1 dc), work 11 dc in the center of the ring, and join with a sl st to the 3rd ch of the starting ch-3 (12 dc). *Rnd 2:* Ch 3 (counts as 1 dc), work 1 dc in the next sp, *2 dc in the next dc, rep from * around, and join with a sl st to the 3rd ch of the starting ch-3 (24 dc). *Rnd 3:* Ch 6, *skip 1 dc, work 1 dc in the next dc, ch 3, rep from * around, and join with a sl st to the 3rd ch of the starting ch-6 (12 ch-3 sps). *Rnd 4:* Ch 3, work (1 tr, 2 dbl tr, 1 tr, and 1 dc) in the next ch-3 sp, *(1 dc, 1 tr, 2 dbl tr, 1 tr, and 1 dc)—one picot made—in the next ch-3 sp, rep from * around, and join with a sl st to the 3rd st of the starting ch-3. Fasten off. To finish each motif, attach yarn to any picot on any motif between the 2 dbl tr's on the last rnd, *ch 6, sc in the next picot, rep from * around, and join with a sl st to the 1st st. *Rnd 2:* Sl st in each of the first 3 ch, sc in the same ch-6 lp, *ch 9, sc in the next ch-6 lp, and end by repeating from * around. Join the rnd with a sl st made in the 1st sc of Rnd 2. *Rnd 3:* Sl st in each of the first 3 ch, sc in the same starting ch-9 lp of Rnd 2, ch 9, sc in the same lp (corner), *(ch 9, sc in the next ch-9 lp) 3 times, ch 9, sc in the same ch-9 lp (another corner), rep from * around, and join with a sl st in the 1st sc of Rnd 3.

Joining: Join the motifs into two strips of seven each. Attach yarn to any corner of any motif, sl st in a corner of the next motif to be joined, *ch 6, sc in the next ch lp on the first motif, ch 6, sc in the next ch lp on the second motif, rep from * twice more, then ch 6, sc in the next ch lp on the first motif, ch 6, and work 1 sl st through the corners of the first and second motifs. Fasten off. Join the two strips as follows: Holding the strips wrong sides together, sl st the 2 corners tog, *ch 6, sc in the next ch-9 lp on the first strip, ch 6, sc in the next ch-9 lp on the second strip, rep from * to the point where the four corners meet, sl st through all 4 lps together, and then rep from * until both strips have been completely joined. End with 1 sl st in both of the last two corners. Fasten off.

Edging: Attach yarn to any corner, ch 3, work 2 dc in the same corner, ch 2, work 3 dc in the same corner, *(6 dc in the next ch lp) 3 times, 3 dc in the next lp, 1 tr c in the joining, 3 dc in the next lp, rep from * to the next corner. Work 3 dc, ch 2, and 3 dc in the corner, and then rep from * around the entire piece. *Next Rnd:* Work 1 dc in each dc and each tr c around and (3 dc, ch 2, and 3 dc) in each corner as you turn. Complete the edging by working 1 rnd of reverse single crochet around the piece, working from left to right instead of right to left and working 3 sc in each corner as you turn.

Finishing: Fold the piece in half lengthwise and sew the edges together with an overcast st, sewing across both short ends and along the long edge from the outer corner through the middle of the third motif at each end so that the center portion is left open for wearing the piece over the head. On the portions that have been joined, sew together the back-to-back motifs (two sets at each end of the wraparound) so that they stay permanently in place.

3

The Pet Toggery

19
The Cat's Sweater

A preening feline will be in his or her glory when outfitted in this soft mohair sweater. The striped sleeves and turtleneck lend a sporty look to the sweater for staying stylishly warm in frosty weather. Knitting is the form of needlework used here, and an unusual vertical pattern emerges from the stitch combination. The project pieces are quickly and easily assembled. Knitted bands anchor the sweater securely, so your pet won't be bothered by the sweater shifting as he or she scampers.

Materials:
3 balls (1 ounce each) Spinnerin Frostlon Petite; 2 balls in aqua (A) and 1
   ball in rust (B)
2 pairs straight knitting needles: #4 and #7
small amount elastic thread

Pattern Stitch: *Row 1:* *K the 2nd st on left-hand needle, k the 1st st, drop
   both sts from left-hand needle, and repeat from * across; *Row 2:* Purl.
   Repeat these 2 rows for pattern.

Gauge in Pattern Stitch: 5 stitches = 1 inch

The Sweater

Top Portion: Starting at the back with A and #4 needles, cast on 40 sts.
Work in k 1, p 1 ribbing for 2 inches. Change to #7 needles and pat st and
work even until piece measures 10 inches. *Next Row:* Bind off 4 sts for leg
opening; work in pat to end of row. Rep last row once more. Then work even
on 32 sts for 2½ inches. Cast on 4 sts now at end of each of the next 2 rows
and work even on 40 sts for 1½ inches more. Change to #4 needles and, alternating 2 rows A and 2 rows B, work in k 1, p 1 ribbing for 3¾ inches. Bind
off loosely in ribbing.

Underneath Portion: With A and #7 needles, cast on 22 sts. Starting with
a purl row, work even in pat for 2½ inches. Bind off 4 sts at beg of each of
the next 2 rows for the leg openings. Work even on 14 sts for 2½ inches; then
cast on 4 sts at the end of each of the next 2 rows. Work even now on 22 sts
for 1½ inches. Change to #4 needles and work the underneath portion of the
collar to correspond to the top portion.

The Back Straps (Make two): With A and #4 needles, cast on 3 sts and
work in k 1, p 1 ribbing for 8½ inches. Bind off.

Finishing: Seam the top portion to the underneath portion on both sides,
sewing from the bound-off edge of the collar to the start of the leg openings.
To make the leg bands, with A and #4 needles, pick up 38 sts around each
opening and work in k 1, p 1 ribbing for 1½ inches, alternating 2 rows A and
2 rows B as on the collar. Seam the lower portion of the sweater and the leg
bands. Sew the back straps in place along each side, from each edge of the
tail portion to the beginning of the underneath portion at the seams. Draw
elastic thread through the first 2 rows of both the top and underneath ribbed
portions.

20
Pet Parade

Flashy enough for strutting, strong enough for mad-dash walks, this fancy collar and leash set is fun to make. Old-fashioned sailor's knots ensure the supple sturdiness of this macramé project, while gaily colored beads accent your workmanship. The collar is adjustable; the dimensions below are for a small size dog (collar circumference is about 12 inches). If your pet is larger, instructions for making a larger size are included in the procedure. The finished leash is about four feet long.

Materials:
78 yards polyolefin or cable cord in orange
54 oval wooden beads, ⅜ inch long, in orange
swivel hook, buckle, and metal D ring
white glue
lining material for the collar (optional)

The Leash

Cut six strands of cord, each 10½ yards long (or 8 times the desired finished length of the leash). Fold each group of three cords in half and attach them to the ring of the swivel hook with a lark's head knot. Make a square knot, using the four center strands as the foundation and each of the two groups of four outer strands as the working cords. *String one bead now on each group of the two outermost cords, make another square knot, and rep from * 7 times. Then make four square knots without bead trim. Complete this portion of the work with approximately a 7½-inch spiral made of half square knots, again using the four cords on each side as the working cords and the center four cords as the foundation cords. To work the center design, work two square knots with the center eight cords and one square knot directly below these with the center four cords. On each side of these three knots, *work toward the center and make six diagonal double half hitches on each side of the center. Then turn the work face down on your working surface and make six diagonal double half hitches on each side, again working toward the center. Return the piece to the right side now and, continuing to work toward the center, make six diagonal double half hitches on each side. String a bead on either side of the leash on the cord next to the outermost cord of the four remaining free cords. Continuing to use the diagonal foundation strands from the last set of diagonal double half hitches and working from the center out toward the sides, make five diagonal double half hitches on each side of the center. Turn the work face down on your working surface again, and **working from the center out toward the side, make six diagonal double half hitches on each side. Return the piece to the right side and rep from **. Make three square knots now on the center four cords with a bead strung on the center two of the four cords between the first and second and the second and third knots and a spiral of ten half square knots on either side. Rep from * once and once again to the point just before when the three square knots on the center four cords were made (with a bead on the center two of the four). Work one square knot now on the center four cords and, directly below that, two square knots on the center eight cords. Complete the piece with a 7½-inch spiral of half square knots, six square knots, eight square knots with beads strung on two of each of the four outer cords as at the start of the leash, and one square knot without beads. Leave a 2-inch space now and then work thirty-four square knots. Finish the piece by folding the last group of thirty-four square knots in half for a handle, working square knots over the 2-inch free space (see diagram). Clip the cords close, glue the

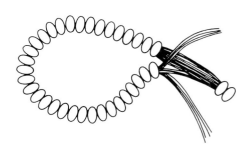

ends in place, and with additional cord, cover those glued ends with a wind-around knot. Make another windaround knot over the dividing point between the four square knots and the last spiral of half square knots.

The Collar

Cut six strands of cord, each 2⅔ yards long, for the collar, which measures approximately 12 inches. If a larger collar is desired, cut each strand 8 times the desired finished length. Fold each cord in half individually over the center bar of the buckle. Make four square knots, adding an additional one at each end of the collar for every extra inch of length necessary. Work the center design in the same manner as the center design on the leash, adding the metal D ring in the center of the design with a double half hitch knot. Complete the collar by making three or more square knots as required; three lark's head knots, each made with six strands (thus forming a center hole for the buckle); one more square knot; one more buckle hole; and, finally, two square knots. Clip the ends of the cords close, and glue the cut ends in place on the wrong side of the piece. If desired, cut lining material to fit and sew it to the collar.

21
A Special Blanket and Bed Pillow
for "Our Friend"

Man's best friend will know you're his best friend when you hook this cozy coverlet and bed pillow for him. The latchet-hooking technique used to make these pieces yields a plush pile meant for pure creature comfort. And visions of doggie bones will dance in his head as he gazes at the crocheted bone appliqués. The pillow is made to fit a small oval bed measuring about 20 by 24 inches; the coverlet is made to that size also. If your dog needs a larger bed, simply start with larger pieces of rug canvas. You can color-coordinate the bed to the pillow and blanket, as we did, by painting the bed a color to match the yarn you're using.

Above: *The Cat's Sweater, p. 64.*
Right: *A Special Blanket and Bed Pillow for "Our Friend," p. 69;*
A Patchwork Denim Walking Coat, p. 73.

70

Pedro's Night "Cover-Up," p. 76.

Materials:

34 packs (320 pieces each) Columbia-Minerva precut rug yarn in copper (MC)

1 skein (2 ounces) Columbia-Minerva Nantuk Bulky in beige (A) and a small amount in wood brown (B)

2 pieces rug canvas, 4 spaces to 1 inch: one piece 21 × 25 inches for the pillow and a second piece 24 × 29 inches for the blanket

latchet hook

aluminum crochet hook: size G

2¼ yards lining material, 36 inches wide, in rust

oval wicker dog bed, approximately 20 × 24 inches, and a foam pillow form cut to fit the inside

1 zipper, 20 inches long

yarn needle

The Pillow

Trace around the outer contour of the pillow form on the rug canvas, add 1 inch all around for trimming and hemming, and then knot one strand of MC yarn in each space, excluding the 1-inch hemming allowance. When the entire piece has been hooked, turn the unworked canvas to the wrong side and hem it in place. Then cut two pieces of lining material to the shape of the finished piece, leaving an extra ¾ inch all around for hemming. Use one of the lining pieces to line the back of the finished work and the remaining piece to make the underneath portion of the pillow. Sew the two pieces together, right sides out, leaving a 20-inch opening for the zipper. Sew in the zipper and insert the pillow form.

Trimming: To make the smallest bone, ch 7 with A, work 1 sc in the 2nd ch from hook and in each of the next 5 ch, ch 1, and turn. *Next Row:* Work a *sc, dc, sc, and sl st* in the 1st st, sl st across each of the next 4 sts, and rep from between *'s in the last st. Continuing around the opposite side of the piece, rep the last row. Join and fasten off. Make the next size bone in the same manner, this time working on a chain of 9 sts and slipping across 6 sts on either side of the piece instead of 4. The remaining two sizes are also worked in the same manner, the next one starting with 11 ch, working on 10 sc for 2 rows, slipping across 8 sts on each side of the piece, and then working a sl st at both short ends between the 2 rows. Start the last bone with 13 ch, work on 12 sc for 3 rows, sl st across 10 sts on each side, and work 2 sl sts at both short ends between the 3 rows. When all four bones are complete, embroider markings on them with Color B, using a running back stitch along each short end as shown and french knots in between. Then sew them in place on the pillow, positioning them as shown in the photograph.

The Blanket

Work in MC yarn as you did for the pillow. When the piece is completely hooked, turn the unworked 1-inch border under, sew it down, cut lining material to fit, and attach it. The one large bone used to trim this piece is made in the same way as the smaller bone except that this one is started with 15 ch, worked on 14 sc for 4 rows, slip stitched across 12 sts on each side, and then slip stitched across 3 sts at both short ends between the 4 rows. Embroider the markings along each end of this bone with a Color B running back stitch, as for the smaller ones, and then, with the same stitch, embroider the dog's name or initials, working the letters according to the alphabet chart on page 8.

22
A Patchwork Denim Walking Coat

A sporty knitted coat that you can make in less than a weekend will keep your pet toasty warm during winter walks. If your pet's even slightly sociable, he'll bask in all the attention his coat attracts for him with its very current denim-look yarn, knitted patchwork, shawl collar, and silver buttons. The ingenious styling of this coat, which measures 15 inches in length, allows you to adjust the coat to fit your particular dog simply by placing the buttons closer to or farther away from the edges of the undersection of the coat. A single crochet stitch borders the coat for an easy, smooth finish.

Materials:

2 skeins (4 ounces each) Reynolds Reynelle knitting worsted in green
     heather (MC) and small amounts of tropical sun (A) and horizon (B)
straight knitting needles: #10
aluminum crochet hook: size F
tapestry needle: #18
4 silver buttons, approximately ¾ inch in diameter

Pattern Stitch: *Row 1 (right side):* Purl; *Row 2:* Knit. Repeat these 2 rows for
     pattern.

Gauge: 4 stitches = 1 inch, using double strands of yarn

The Coat

Top Portion: With double strands of MC and working in pat st throughout,
cast on 12 sts. Work 2 rows even; then inc 2 sts at the end of every row until
there are 40 sts. Then inc 1 st at beg and end of every other row until there
are 48 sts. Work even for 4 rows; on the next row, inc 1 st at beg and end.
Work even now on 50 sts for 15 rows. On the next row, form the buttonholes
in the following manner: K 3, bind off 3, k to within the last 6 sts, then bind
off 3 sts and k to the end of the row. On the next row, cast on 3 sts over each
set of 3 bound off on the previous row. Work 2 rows even. Then dec 1 st at
beg and end of every other row 3 times. Work even on 44 sts for 3 inches
more. Then inc 1 st at beg and end of every other row 3 times. Work even
on 50 sts for 2 rows. To shape the top, k 3, bind off the next 3 sts (for another
buttonhole), k 6, sl remaining sts on a holder. *Next Row:* Work across 6 sts,
cast on 3 sts over those bound off on previous row, and k the remaining 3
sts. Dec 1 st at beg of every other row 3 times; bind off remaining 6 sts. Leaving the 26 center sts on a holder, shape the other side of the top to correspond.

The Collar: Knit the 26 sts from the holder, knit the next row, and then, reversing the stockinette st pat, work as follows: Work 1 row even, dec 1 st at
beg and end of next row, work 8 rows even, dec 1 st at beg and end of next
row, work 4 rows even, and dec 1 st at beg and end of next row. Bind off
loosely the remaining 20 sts.

The Underneath Portion: With double strands of MC and working in pat st,
cast on 28 sts. Work 1 row even, inc 1 st at beg and end of next row, and
work 3 rows even. Dec 1 st now at beg and end of every other row 7 times
and then every 4th row twice. Work even on 16 sts until entire piece measures 7½ inches. Dec 1 st at beg and end of next row, work 1 row even, and
bind off.

The Patches: *The Collar Patch:* *With a single strand of MC, cast on 6 sts,
k 1 row, and p 1 row. Then k 2 rows with A, k 1 row and p 1 row with B, k
1 row and p 1 row with MC, *k 2 rows with A, k 1 row and p 1 row with B,
and k 1 row and p 1 row with MC; bind off. *Smallest Body Patch:* Repeat instructions between *'s on the collar patch and bind off. *Diamond-shaped
Patch:* With a single strand of A, cast on 10 sts and work throughout in seed
st (k 1, p 1 across the row; then k the sts that were knitted on the previous
row and p the sts that were purled on the previous row). Work 1 row even.
On next row, dec 1 st at beg and inc 1 st at the end; rep these 2 rows until
piece measures 2 inches. Bind off. *Large Square Patch:* With a single strand
of MC, cast on 10 sts. *Row 1:* k 1, *k 1, sl 1 as if to p, rep from * across row,
and end k 1. *Row 2:* With MC, k 1, *sl 1 as if to p, k 1, rep from * across row,

and end k 2. *Row 3:* With B, k 1, *sl 1 as if to p, k 1, rep from * across row, and end k 2. *Row 4:* With B, k 1, *k 1, sl 1 as if to p, rep from * across row, ending k 1. Rep this pat until piece measures 2½ inches. Bind off.

Finishing: With double strands of MC and with right side of work facing, work 2 rows of sc completely around the top (including the collar) and underneath portions of the coat, rounding out the corners and having the balance of the work lie flat. Now work a 3rd row, this time in reverse, working the sc from left to right instead of right to left. Fasten off. With a single strand of A, embroider an outline stitch along all edges, placing these stitches just within the first round of sc. Sew on the patches as shown in the photograph or as desired, using the wrong side of each patch as the right side.

The Ladybug Trim: *Body:* With a single strand of A, ch 3 for the body and join with a sl st to form a ring. Work 10 sc in the center of the ring. On the next rnd, work 2 sc in each sc around. Work 1 rnd even on 20 sts and fasten off. *Head:* Ch 3 and join with a sl st to form a ring. Work 6 sc in the center of the ring, ch 1, and turn. *Next Rnd:* Work 2 sc in each sc around. Join and fasten off. With MC, embroider an outline st down the middle of the body portion and two french knots along each side of the center line. Sew the body in place as shown in the photograph, sew the head in position on top of the body, and with a Color A outline stitch, embroider six straight legs and two curved tentacles.

To complete the coat, finish the buttonholes with an overcast st and sew the buttons on to correspond to them.

23
Pedro's Night "Cover-Up"

A crocheted night cover outshines the usual plastic cover or towel as a bird-cage cover. This useful and attractive accessory embroidered with a vivid parrot motif also has room to add to it your bird's name. Fringe and contrasting contour stitching accent the main pieces, which are worked in afghan stitch (see Chapter 7 for easy instructions). The finished piece will fit any standard-size bird-cage that stands about 15 inches high. When you make this piece, you'll be adding a nice, decorative touch to a room as well as pampering a favorite feathered friend.

Materials:

10 balls (175 yards each) J. & P. Coats "Knit-Cro-Sheen" in pongee (MC)
10 skeins (12 yards each) Red Heart Persian Type needlepoint and crewel
    yarn: 5 skeins in rusticana #205 (A) and 1 skein each in light turquoise
    #738, chartreuse #550, dark orange #968, olive #510, and daffodil #044
aluminum afghan hook: size I
aluminum crochet hook: size E
crewel needle: #4

Gauge in Afghan Stitch: 4 stitches = 1 inch; 4 double rows = 1 inch, using
    double strands of yarn

The Cover

Back: Working in afghan stitch and with double strands of yarn, ch 81 with MC. Work even on 80 sts for 1 inch and then dec 1 st at beg and end of next row. Rep this dec every 4th row 4 times more, then every other row 6 times, and every row 5 times (48 sts). Dec 2 sts now at beg and end of each of the next 2 rows. Continuing to dec on every row, dec 3 sts at beg and end of each of the next 2 rows, 4 sts at beg and end of the next row, and 5 sts at beg and end of the next row. When 42 rows have been worked and 10 sts remain, fasten off.

Side Panels (Make two pieces): Ch 39 and work even on 38 sts for 66 rows. Fasten off.

Left Front: Ch 45 and work even on 44 sts for 1 inch. Dec 1 st at end of next row, work 3 rows even, and rep this dec at end of next row. Continuing to dec at side edge only, dec 1 st every other row 12 times, 1 st every row 3 times, then 2 sts at the side edge of each of the next 2 rows, 3 sts on each of the next 2 rows, and 4 sts on each of the next 3 rows. When 5 sts remain and piece measures same length as back, fasten off.

Right Front: Work to correspond to the left front, reversing the shaping.

Finishing: With double strands of MC, work 1 row of sc along the outer edges of each of the five pieces, working 3 sts in each corner st as you turn, rounding out the curve-shaped portions, and having the rest of the work lie flat. Join the pieces, leaving the two front sections open at the center, with a row of sl st worked on the right side of the piece. Work 2 rows of sc around the remaining unjoined outer edges. With double strands of A, embroider cross-stitches over each joining seam, making these sts large enough to cover the seam completely; then go on to cross-stitch along the two center front edges and around the neck opening. With triple strands of A, make two 10-inch-long twisted cords for the front ties and sew these in place as shown in the photograph. Then, following the chart for color and design, embroider each front as indicated, using single strands of yarn and a cross-stitch just large enough to cover each afghan-stitch square. Add the name of your bird in the blank area on the right front, following the alphabet chart given on page 8. Finish the piece by cutting a number of 5½-inch-long strands of MC and knot three strands in each st around the bottom of the cover.

left front

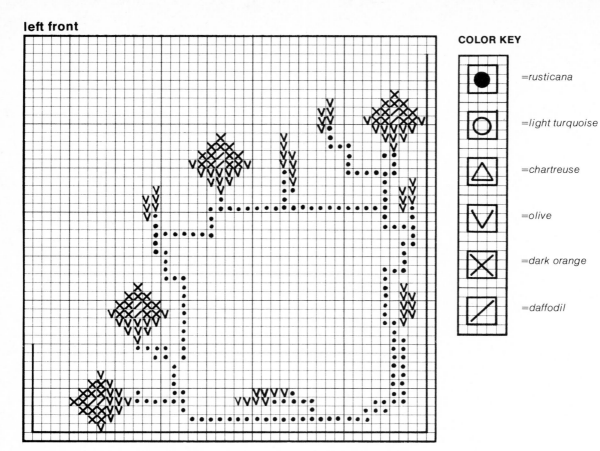

COLOR KEY

●	=*rusticana*
○	=*light turquoise*
△	=*chartreuse*
∨	=*olive*
⊠	=*dark orange*
⧄	=*daffodil*

right front

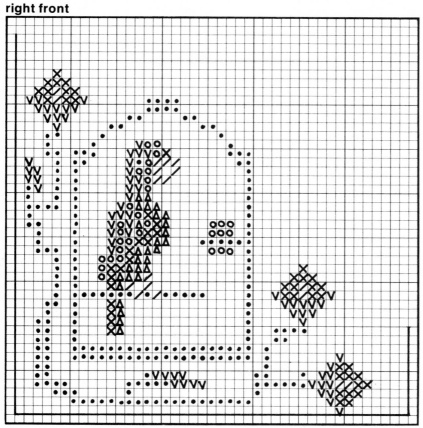

4

the
needlework boutique

The Something Special Shop for Him

24
A Striped Tie

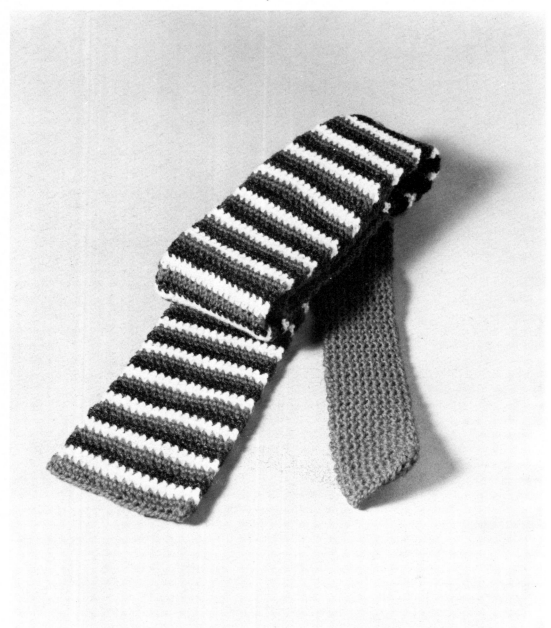

The striped tie, worked in a simple single crochet stitch, is a welcome accessory for any man. Made in jewel red, white, and charcoal gray, it is very much in style today and will complement his gray pinstriped suit beautifully. It's a great year-round gift, and you can complete it in about half a day. This attractive tie may well turn out to be the favorite one in his wardrobe.

Materials:
4 balls (50 grams each) Reynolds Classique: 2 balls in jewel red (MC) and
    1 ball each in white (A) and charcoal gray (B)
aluminum crochet hook: size F

Gauge in Single Crochet: 6 stitches = 1 inch; 7 rows = 1 inch

The Tie

Make two pieces: With MC, ch 19 and work 2 rows of sc on 18 sts. Then, working on these sts, work 2 rows with A and then 2 rows with B. Alternate 2 rows MC, 2 rows A, and 2 rows B until piece measures 15 inches. Continuing with the striped pattern, dec 1 st now at beg and end of the next row; rep this dec every 2 inches 3 times more. Break off A and B and then continue working with MC until piece measures 48 inches in all. Fasten off.

Finishing: Sew the two pieces together, right sides out, being careful to match the pattern on the striped portion of the tie.

Top, from left to right: *Slipper Sandals, p. 91; His Best Scarf, p. 88; Driving Gloves, p. 93; The Turtleneck, p. 86; Executive Socks, p. 83; A Striped Tie, p. 80.* Above: *His Name Plate, with a Coordinating Desk Set, p. 95.*

25
Executive Socks

These knitted, mid-calf-length socks will provide the finishing touch to his business suit or leisure outfit. They are worked in a sophisticated tweed pattern of charcoal heather, scarlet, and white with deep, solid-colored toes, heels, and ribbed tops, making for a particularly striking look. Worked in an easy-to-follow pattern stitch, the socks are interesting to make, and he'll enjoy hours of comfort in them. They're machine washable, too.

Materials:
4 skeins (1 ounce each) Bernat Berella 3-ply fingering yarn: 2 skeins in char-
     coal heather (MC) and 1 skein each in scarlet (A) and white (B)
2 pairs straight knitting needles: #3 and #7
double-pointed knitting needles: #3
2 stitch holders

Pattern Stitch: *Row 1:* With A, *k 1, sl 1 as if to p, rep from * across the row;
     Row 2: With B, *p 1, sl 1 as if to k, rep from * across the row. Repeat Rows
     1 and 2 for the pattern, alternating colors MC, A, and B and changing
     color on every row.

Gauge in Pattern Stitch: 7 stitches = 1 inch on #7 needles

The Socks

Make two: With MC and #3 needles, loosely cast on 60 sts. Work in k 1, p
1 ribbing for 1½ inches. Purl the last row and inc 8 sts evenly spaced on
this row. Change to #7 needles and pat st, and work even until piece measures 10½ inches in all. Then start the heel: Sl the first 17 sts onto a #3 needle, place the next 34 sts on a stitch holder, and sl the last 17 sts onto
another #3 needle. With wrong side of work facing you, bring the two 17-st sections around to the front so that they are next to each other and can be
worked as a single piece to form the heel; then transfer the sts onto one needle. With MC and the right side of work facing, k the next row, decreasing
4 sts evenly spaced on this row. Then shape the back of the heel: With the
wrong side of the work facing you, sl 1 as if to p and then p across the row.
Row 2: *Sl 1 as if to p, k 1, rep from * across the row. Rep these 2 rows until
32 rows have been worked, ending with Row 2.

Heel: With wrong side of work facing you, sl 1 as if to p, p 16, p 2 tog, p
1, and turn. *Next Row:* Sl 1 as if to k, k 5, sl 1 as if to k, k 1, psso, k 1, and
turn. *Next Row:* Sl 1 as if to p, p 6, p 2 tog, p 1, and turn. *Next Row:* Sl 1
as if to k, k 7, sl 1 as if to k, k 1, psso, k 1, and turn. Continue in this way,
working 1 more st between the decreases on each row until all the sts have
been worked, ending with a knit row. There will be 18 sts on the needle.

Gusset: With MC and a dp needle, pick up 16 sts along one finished edge
of the heel. Purl these sts and then purl the 18 sts on the needle; with a spare
needle, pick up 16 sts along the other finished side of the heel. Divide the
50 sts onto the 2 dp needles, 25 on each one, and then, with the right side
of work facing, work as follows: *Row 1:* K 1, sl 1, k 1, psso, and k to the end
of the needle. Then, working across the other needle, k to within the last 3
sts, k 2 tog, k 1. *Row 2:* Purl. Rep these 2 rows until 14 sts remain on each
needle.

Sole: Sl the 28 sts onto a #3 straight needle and then, with MC, work in
stockinette st until the piece measures 2 inches less than the desired length,
ending with a purl row. Sl these sts onto a holder.

Instep: Sl the 34 sts from the first holder onto a #7 needle and, decreasing 1
st at beg and end of the first row, continue working in pat st as established
until piece measures the same length as the sole, ending with a purl row. Sl
these sts onto a dp needle.

Toe: Divide the 28 sole sts onto 2 dp needles, and sl 1 st from each side
of the center needle onto each needle. There are now 15 sts on each of the
two needles and 30 instep sts on a third needle. Now shape the toe as fol-

lows: Working with MC only, k to within 3 sts of the first needle, k 2 tog, k 1; on the second needle, k 1, sl 1, k 1, psso, k to within the last 3 sts, k 2 tog, k 1; and on the third needle, k 1, sl 1 as if to k, k 1, psso, k to the end of the needle. *Next Rnd:* Purl. Rep these 2 rnds until 16 sts remain—4 sts on the first and third needles and 8 sts on the second needle. Work across the 4 sts on the first needle now and sl them onto the third needle. You now have 16 sts, 8 on each of two needles. Break off the yarn, leaving a 20-inch thread to weave together the toe sts. Then sew all open seams.

26
The Turtleneck

This quick-to-knit turtleneck is an all-purpose handy wardrobe stretcher for many occasions. It can be used as a sweater, a dickie, or a vest, and can be worn under a jacket, under a shirt, or even over a shirt. Directions are written for a small size (36–38). Changes for a medium size (40–42) and a large size (44–46) follow in parentheses. It's the perfect gift for the man on the go, and it takes less than a day to make!

Materials:
6 (8,10) skeins (1 ounce each) Spinnerin Genie in red #6250
2 pairs straight knitting needles: #8 and #11

Gauge in Stockinette Stitch: 3 stitches = 1 inch

The Turtleneck

Back: With #8 needles, cast on 54 (60,66) sts. K 1, p 1 in ribbing for 3 inches. Bind off 11 (12,13) sts at beg of each of the next 2 rows. Then change to #11 needles and stockinette st and work even on 32 (36,40) sts until entire piece measures 23½ (24½,25) inches. Bind off 7 (9,11) sts at beg of the next 2 rows and then bind off loosely the remaining 18 sts for the back of the neck.

Front: Work same as for back until piece measures 21½ (22½,23) inches. Then shape neck: Work across 10 (12,14) sts, join another ball of yarn, bind off loosely the center 12 sts, and then work across the remaining 10 (12,14) sts. Working on both sides at once, dec 1 st at each neck edge every other row 3 times. Then work even on 7 (9,11) sts of each side until piece measures same as back to shoulder; bind off.

Finishing: Sew one shoulder seam. Then with #8 needles and the right side of the work facing, pick up and k 38 (40,42) sts around the neck. K 1, p 1 in ribbing on these sts for 5 inches and then bind off loosely. Sew collar and remaining open shoulder seam, and sew the bottom waistband seams.

27
His Best Scarf

For the winter season, make him this smartly styled knitted scarf. Striped in charcoal and white, the scarf can be worn with his business attire or sports clothes. It's richly lined in silk in a contrasting color, but even more important, it is personalized with his own three-letter monogram. This is truly a very special gift for a very special person.

Materials:

5 skeins (1 ounce each) Brunswick Fairhaven 3-ply fingering yarn: 3 skeins in charcoal (MC) and 1 skein each in white (A) and cardinal (B)

straight knitting needles: #5

aluminum crochet hook: size E

embroidery needle

⅜ yard lining material, 48 inches wide, in cardinal

Reverse Stockinette Stitch: *Row 1 (right side):* Purl; *Row 2:* Knit. Repeat these 2 rows for pattern.

Gauge in Pattern Stitch: 6 stitches = 1 inch; 8 rows = 1 inch

The Scarf

With MC, cast on 288 sts. Work even in pat st for 6 rows, break off MC, attach A, and work as follows: *Row 7:* Knit. *Row 8:* Purl. Break off A and, with MC, work as follows: *Row 9:* Knit. *Row 10:* Knit. Repeat Rows 3 through 10 until eleven Color A stripes have been worked, ending the piece with 6 more rows of MC; *at the same time,* follow the color and stitch key on the chart for the monogrammed portion of the scarf, using whichever initials you wish from the alphabet chart appearing on page 8 and doubling both their width and length. (*Note:* When changing from stockinette st to reverse stockinette st involving a change of color too, the first row of the new color must be knitted; then the reverse stockinette may be continued in the usual manner.)

Finishing: Block the scarf with a warm iron over a damp cloth. Then with double strands of A, embroider a running chain-stitch stripe over each Color A stripe, working each chain stitch over two knitted stitches. (*Note:* Because of the nature of the pat st, the work may not lie perfectly flat even after the first blocking; however, this problem will have been eliminated after the embroidered chain stitches have been worked.) With MC, work 2 rows of sc along each long edge of the scarf; then with double strands of MC, embroider a running chain stitch over these sc rows. Work 2 rows of color-over-color sc along each short edge of the scarf. For fringe, cut 4½-inch strands of MC and Color A, and, using color over color, knot four strands in each st along each short edge of the scarf. Block the piece once more; then cut the lining material to fit and sew it on.

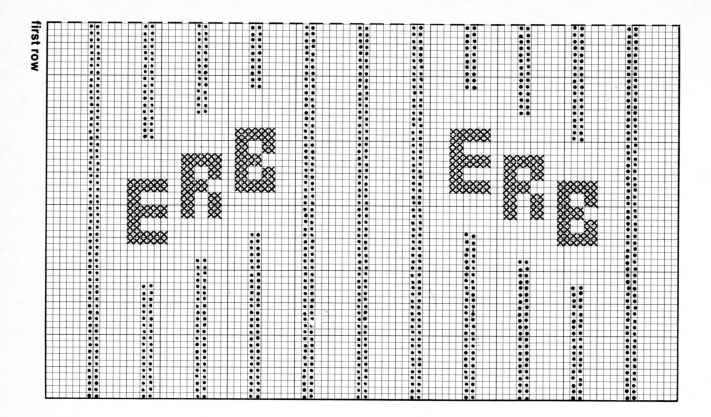

COLOR and STITCH KEY

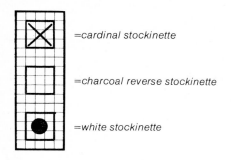

=cardinal stockinette

=charcoal reverse stockinette

=white stockinette

90

28
Slipper Sandals

This pair of slipper sandals, a comfortable accessory for relaxing any time, will also make a fine addition to his summer wardrobe. Creating these easy-to-wear sandals requires nothing more than a little time, a crochet hook, one skein of yarn, two pairs of innersoles, and a little glue and elastic. Directions are written for a man's size small. Changes for medium and large sizes follow in parentheses. Make the sandals for his birthday, Father's Day, or even Christmas—they're a gift for all seasons!

Materials:

1 ball (3½ ounces) Unger's Roly-Poly in natural
aluminum crochet hook: size G
2 pairs men's foam latex innersoles in proper size
1¼ yards elastic, ¾ inch wide
Duco cement or other nonsoluble glue

Gauge in Single Crochet: 9 stitches = 2 inches

The Sandals

Long Strips (Make two): Ch 89 (93,97) and work in sc on 88 (92,96) sts for 1½ inches. Fasten off.

Short Strips (Make four): Ch 45 (49,53) and work in sc on 44 (48,52) sts for 1½ inches. Fasten off.

Finishing: To finish one slipper, mark the center point of one long strip. Then, holding two of the innersoles together, right sides out, glue the marked center point of one long strip between the two soles, placing it at a point approximately 2 inches in from the toe end. When this strip is securely in place, crisscross the ends on top of the sole and then glue the two short ends together, again between the two innersoles, at a point approximately 4 inches in from the heel end. Glue the two innersole pieces together now, being generous with the glue and, if possible, clamping with C-clamps, hair clips, or clothespins during the drying process. Then cut two pieces of elastic, each to the length of one of the short strips. Sew the two ends of each piece of elastic to the two ends of each of the now-crisscrossed long strips at the top of the slipper. Finally, sew two of the short strips over the two strips of elastic. To trim each top strip, crochet three chains with double strands of yarn, each approximately 14 inches long. Braid these chains and then sew them along the center of the top strip, cutting off any excess length. Tack the two strips together at the point of crossing. Construct the other slipper in the same manner.

29
Driving Gloves

Driving gloves, whether for driving or all-around winter wear, make a perfect gift. Crocheted in dark gray, these particular gloves have their areas of greatest wear protected with leather patches. If you prefer more of a dress-wear appearance, line the gloves with suede. If the gloves are intended for everyday use, select a sturdy plastic material. The crochet stitch used for these gloves makes them durable and enables them to hold their shape well. This welcome gift is one that will last for years.

Materials:

2 balls (1.4 ounces each) Unger Cruise in dark gray #67
aluminum crochet hook: size E
dark gray suede, leather, or plastic material, 8 × 10 inches, for lining

Gauge in Single Crochet: 11 stitches = 2 inches

The Gloves

Right Glove: Ch 31 for the palm section and, working in sc throughout, work even on 30 sts until piece measures 3 inches. Then shape the thumb: Ch 9 at the end of the last row and turn. *Next Row:* Sc in the 2nd ch from hook and in each of the next 7 ch, sc in each of the next 10 sc, ch 1, and turn. Work even on 18 sts until piece measures 2½ inches, or ½ inch less than the desired thumb length, and then shape the top: Work 2 sts tog across the row (9 sts). *Next 2 Rows:* Work 1 sc in the 1st st and then work 2 sts tog across the row (3 sts). Break off yarn, leaving a 6-inch thread; sew the thumb seam with the thread. To complete the palm, return to the row where the thumb was started, attach the yarn in the 1st ch of the foundation ch for the thumb, and, working along the opposite edge of that chain, work across the remaining 7 thumb sts. Continuing across the palm sts, work the next 2 sts tog and work 1 st in each of the remaining 18 sts (26 sts in all). Work even on these sts until piece measures 5 inches from the very start, ending at the outer edge. Then shape the little finger: Sc across 5 sts, ch 3, and turn. Work even on 7 sc for 2¼ inches, or ½ inch less than the desired length, and then shape the top: Skip the 1st st, then work 2 sc tog across the row, and fasten off. Shape the ring finger: Attach yarn to the st next to those on which the little finger was worked, sc across 6 sts, ch 3, and turn. Work even on 8 sts for 3 inches, or ½ inch less than the desired length, work 2 sc tog across the row, and fasten off. Shape the middle finger: Attach yarn to the st next to those on which the ring finger was worked, work across 7 sts, ch 3, and turn. Work even on 9 sts for 3½ inches, or ½ inch less than the desired length. On the next row, skip 1 st, work 2 sts tog across the row, and fasten off. Shape the index finger: Attach yarn to the st next to those on which the middle finger was worked, sc across 8 sts, and inc 1 st in the last st. Work even on 9 sts as for the middle finger, shape the top in the same way as the other fingers, and fasten off. To make the back section, ch 27 and work in sc on 26 sts until piece measures 5 inches. Then shape the fingers as on the palm section.

Left Glove: Work to correspond to the right glove, reversing the shaping.

Finishing: Sew finger and side seams. To make two ribbed cuffs, ch 11 for each cuff and work in sc through the back lps only of 10 sts for 8 inches. Sew one cuff to each glove, joining the short ends at the outside side seams. To line the gloves, cut six pieces from the lining material to measure ⅝ inch wide by 2¼ inches long (for the thumbs, index fingers, and ring fingers), two to measure ⅝ inch wide by 2¾ inches long (for the middle fingers), and two to measure ⅝ inch wide by 1½ inches long for the little fingers. Round the corners of these pieces and sew them in place on the outside of the fingers on the palm side. For the palms, cut two rectangles, each 1¼ inches by 3¾ inches, and sew one across the palm of each glove.

30
His Name Plate,
with a Coordinating Desk Set

For a handsome, decorative touch, make him this good-looking three-piece set—blotter, pencil holder, and name plate—for his desk. Simply crocheted in scarlet, charcoal heather, and white, the set is easily assembled. Work it up in the striped pattern stitch with all three colors, or use one skein of each color for each part of the set. Either way, this desk set will be a welcome daily reminder of your thoughtfulness.

Materials:

6 skeins (1 ounce each) Bernat Berella 3-ply fingering yarn: 2 skeins each in scarlet (A), charcoal heather (B), and white (C)

aluminum crochet hook: size F

tapestry needle: #18

1 piece heavy cardboard, 16 × 27 inches, for desk pad

2 pieces felt: one 16 × 27 inches, for desk pad, and one 3½ × 9½ inches, for name plate, in white

½ sheet poster paper, 22 × 28 inches, for name plate

1 frozen-juice-concentrate can, 12-ounce size, for pencil holder

masking tape, 1 inch wide

double-faced masking tape, 1 inch wide

desk blotter, 19 × 24 inches

Striped Pattern Stitch: *Row 1:* With B, work in sc across the row, attach C, draw through last B lp on hook, drop B, ch 1 with C, and turn. *Row 2:* With C, work in sc across the row; drop the last lp from the hook, and do not turn the work. *Row 3:* *Return to start of row, insert hook into the top lp of the first Color C st, pick up B and draw it through, and then with B, work in sc across the row. Pick up the Color C lp, draw it through the last Color B lp on the hook, drop B, ch 1, and turn. *Row 4:* With C, work in sc across the row. Drop C, and do not turn. Repeat from * for the striped pattern stitch.

Gauge in Single Crochet: 9 stitches = 2 inches, using double strands of yarn

The Name Plate

Front: With double strands of B, ch 47. Working in sc throughout, work even on 46 sts for 5 rows. *Next Row:* Work across 5 sts with B, attach C, and work to within the last 5 sts. Attach another ball of B and work the last 5 sts with B. Work color over color now for 6 rows. Then break off C and work in B only for 5 more rows; fasten off.

Back: With double strands of B, ch 47. Work even in sc on 46 sts for 17 rows. Fasten off.

Side Insertions (Make two pieces): With double strands of B, ch 16. Working in sc throughout, work even on 15 sts for 1 row. Then dec 1 st at beg and end of the next row and rep this dec at beg and end of every other row until 1 st remains. Fasten off.

Finishing: With four strands of A and a cross-stitch, embroider the desired name or initials, following the alphabet chart on page 8 and fitting the letters into the Color C stripe on the front strip. Then with double strands of Color C, crochet a chain to fit around the four sides of the Color C stripe and sew it in place. With right sides out now, join the front strip to the back strip along the top edge only with a row of sc, using double strands of B. Then fit one triangular side insertion in place between each of the two sides of the now partially joined front and back pieces and join these with a row of sc, again using double strands of B. Work 1 row of sc around the entire bottom edge of the joined piece with double strands of B. Then with double strands of A, work a row of sc around this edge, across the top, and along the two joining edges on each side.

To complete the piece, cut five pieces of poster paper, three to measure 3 by 9½ inches (for front, back, and bottom of the name plate) and two to measure the size and shape of the triangular side insertions. Securely tape these pieces together to form the shape of the plate and then slip the finished crocheted piece over the cardboard form. Cut a piece of felt to the size of the bottom of the form and sew this in place along the four sides of the bottom of the piece, sewing it to the four bottom edges of the crocheted piece.

The Pencil Holder

Using double strands of yarn throughout and Color A, ch 21. Work even in sc on 20 sts for 4 rows. Break off A, attach B, and work in the striped pat st until nineteen Color C and twenty Color B stripes have been completed. Fasten off.

Finishing: Work 1 row of color-over-color sc along the right side of each of the two long edges of the strip and then work 1 row of Color A along each of these edges. Sew the last Color B row to the first Color A row, and then slip the completed piece over the empty juice can, holding it securely in place with a strip of double-faced tape around the center of the can.

The Desk Pad

Side Strips (Make two pieces): Using double strands of yarn and sc throughout, ch 87 with A. Work even on 86 sts for 4 rows. Fasten off A, attach B, and work in the striped pat until 4 rows of C and 5 rows of B have been completed. Fasten off B and C, attach double strands of A, work 1 row of sc and fasten off. Turn work and work 5 rows of the striped pat and 1 row of color A sc along the opposite side of the strip.

Finishing: Stretch each crocheted strip along each short edge of the 16- by 27-inch piece of cardboard, folding to the underside the ends of the crocheted pieces, half at the top and half at the bottom of the cardboard piece. Tape these ends in place. Place the 16- by 27-inch piece of felt over the cardboard so that it covers the top and bottom turned-under edges of the two crocheted strips at each end. Tape the felt in place over the top and bottom edges only, omitting the four corners where the crocheted ends were turned under. Sew the two long edges and the four turned-under corner edges of the crocheted strips to the corresponding felt edges. Cut the blotter to fit the finished piece now and slide it under each crocheted strip, running a 16-inch strip of double-faced tape between the blotter and the crocheted strip on each side in order to hold the blotter securely in place.

5

the
needlework boutique

The
Handcrafted
Home Shop

From left to right: *The Placemat, Shaped as an*
Octagon, p.102 ; For Exotic House Plants, p. 100 .

31
For Exotic House Plants

Welcome spring into your home with this most attractive and easy-to-make macramé plant hanger. All you need is some heavy wrapping twine to create this exotic plant paradise, which will brighten any corner of any room. Stretching from ceiling to floor, it does double-duty, for it accommodates two potted plants, a large one at the bottom and a smaller one on top. Above the smaller pot is a decorative spiral loop to suspend from a ceiling hook. Dress up a bay window, or make it for someone special for his new home.

Material:
125 yards of heavy wrapping twine

The Plant Hanger

Cut nine 25-foot lengths of twine, fold them in half (possibly around the leg of a heavy table or chair), and draw all ends to an even length. Cut an additional strand to measure 50 feet, and fold this one so that 9 feet of its additional length are on the left side and 16 feet are on the right side. Finally, cut one more strand to measure 3 feet, folding it too along with the others. Maintaining all the strands in this position and using the longer end of the 50-foot strand as the working cord around all the other strands, make a 10-inch length of vertical clove hitches. Start these knots 5 inches from the center point, work toward the center point, and continue for 5 inches beyond it. Now cross the eleven strands hanging from the end of the group of clove hitches over the eleven strands from the beginning and, using the two ends of the 50-foot strand as the working cords, make a 5-inch spiral of half square knots, using all the remaining unworked strands as the foundation. Let any excess from the 3-foot strand hang free (at even lengths at each end). These free ends will be used for tying later. To make the large outer basket, divide the twenty strands now into five groups of four strands each and work 2 inches of half square knots on each of the five groups. Then, *leaving 3 inches of all strands unworked, work five groups of three square knots; repeat from * until eight groups of square knots have been worked on the five groups of four strands each. Leave 7 inches of all strands unworked and start the lower basket. Using two strands from one group with two strands from the adjacent group, make a series of three square knots on each of the five new groups. Leave 7 inches unworked again and tie all twenty strands into a large slip knot. Trim all free ends 2 inches below the knot.

Start the small inner basket by cutting four 6-foot-long strands of twine and another four that are 18 feet. Place one of the long strands on each side of two of the short strands. Find the center, and at this point, using the longer outside strands as working cords, make three consecutive square knots. Continuing with just the four strands, leave 3 inches unworked, make another group of three square knots, and continue in this manner until four groups of three square knots each have been made after the center one. Pick up the four remaining unworked strands now at the other side of the group of center knots and work another four groups of three square knots each in the same way as the first group. Make another strip of nine groups of three square knots each with the four remaining cut strands, working this strip in the same manner as the first strip. Hang the finished long plant basket in position on a hook. Tie the ends of the 3-foot strand that extend from beneath the hanging loop around the crossed section of the two strips for the shorter basket with a series of three square knots. With the four ends of the two knotted strips hanging now, leave 3 inches free of the unworked portion at the top of each of these free. Then *make a group of three square knots, using two strands from the bottom of one strip and two from the bottom of an adjacent one. This is the start of the smaller hanging basket. To complete this basket, repeat from * 3 times more. Leave 2 inches unworked and then make a large slip knot with all the strands like the one at the bottom of the large basket, trimming the remaining ends of this one to 1½ inches.

32
The Placemat,
Shaped as an Octagon

The octagonal placemat is solid enough to be practical and yet delicate enough to be decorative. It will embellish any formal or informal
table setting, or it can serve as a charming centerpiece. But the true
beauty of it is that you can make it out of nearly any ordinary cord,
such as parcel-post twine. Whether you choose to make it of polished
jute or parcel-post twine, the placemat is exceptionally simple to
make. It is worked in a combination of single crochet and hairpin-lace
stitches, and it can be completed in an afternoon's time.

Materials:
90 yards polished jute or parcel-post twine for each placemat
aluminum crochet hook: size I
adjustable hairpin-lace loom

Gauge in Single Crochet: 3 stitches = 1 inch

The Placemat

Crocheted Section: Starting at the center, ch 2 and then work 6 sc in the 2nd sc from hook. *Next Rnd:* Work 2 sc in each sc around (12 sc). Add a marker to denote start of next and all following rnds. *Next Rnd:* *Work 1 sc in the first sc, 2 sc in the next sc, rep from * around (18 sc). *Next Rnd:* *Work 1 sc in each of the next 2 sc, 2 sc in the next sc, rep from * around (24 sc). Continue in this manner to inc 6 sts evenly spaced on each rnd, allowing on each rnd 1 st more between each point of increase until there are 66 sc in all. Join and fasten off.

Hairpin-Lace Section: With the loom adjusted to 4 inches, make a strip of hairpin lace having 56 lps on each side. To finish one edge of the strip, which will now become the inner edge, *work 1 sc in each of the first 4 lps, work the next 3 lps tog with 1 sc, rep from * 7 times, and then join to the first sc with a sl st and fasten off, leaving a long length with which to sew. On the outer edge, *(sc in the first lp, ch 1) 6 times, work 5 sc in the next lp (one point), ch 1, rep from * 7 times, and then join to the first sc with a sl st in the first sc. Do not fasten off. Continuing around, work as follows: *Next Rnd:* Work 1 sc in each sc and in each ch-1 space, working 3 sc in each point. *Next Rnd:* Working in sl st, work 1 st in each st around. Join the end of this rnd with a sl st in the 1st sl st on the rnd and fasten off.

Finishing: Sew the two ends of the lace strip together, and then sew the inner edge of the strip to the outer edge of the crocheted circle with an overcast stitch, easing in any extra fullness as necessary.

33
An Unusual Hassock

With just four skeins of heavy yarn, a length of fabric, and some cardboard and stuffing material, you can make this handsome hassock. It's a pleasure to have in any home—place it near your favorite chair so that you can rest your feet on it while relaxing or sit right on it. The hairpin lace makes this a decorative piece, too, and it's an easy one to make. Just form rings with hairpin-lace strips, and before the weekend is over, you will have created a unique and functional item to add to your relaxation area.

Materials:

4 balls (4 ounces each) Bernat Berella Bulky in copper
adjustable hairpin-lace loom
aluminum crochet hook: size J
1¾ yards suede cloth, 54 inches wide, in blending or contrasting color
sufficient heavy corrugated cardboard to cut two round pieces, each 19
    inches in diameter, and one long strip, 9 × 60 inches
approximately 25 feet masking tape, 2 or 3 inches wide
Dacron batting, polyfoam, or other stuffing material

Gauge in Half Double Crochet: 3 stitches = 1 inch

The Hassock

Top Center Hairpin-Lace Circle: With the loom adjusted to 4 inches, make a strip having 36 lps on each side. To finish one edge of the strip, which will now become the inner edge, *work 3 lps together with a sl st, rep from * 11 times, join with a sl st to the first sl st to form a ring, and fasten off. Sew the spine ends together. For the outer edge of this circle, *work 3 lps together with a sc, ch 7, rep from * 11 times, join with a sl st to the first sc. Then ch 1 and, continuing around, work 1 hdc in the back lp of each sc and in each ch st around. Join this rnd with a sl st in the first hdc and fasten off.

Top Outer Hairpin-Lace Ring: Again with the loom adjusted to 4 inches, make a strip having 72 lps on each side. Work the inner edge of this ring in the same manner as the outer edge of the center circle, chaining 3 between each sc instead of 7. Work the outer edge in exactly the same manner as the outer edge of the center circle. When this ring has been completed, sew its inner edge to the outer edge of the center circle, using an overcast stitch.

Outside Circumference: Make twelve strips with the loom adjusted to 4 inches, each strip having 24 lps on each side. To finish each side of each strip, *work 3 lps together with a sc, ch 3, rep from * across, then ch 1, and turn. *Next Row:* Work 1 hdc in the front lp only of each sc and each ch st across. Fasten off. Sew the long edges of the twelve strips together to make one long piece, using an overcast stitch.

Finishing: Form the base of the hassock by cutting from the cardboard two circles, each 19 inches in diameter, one to be used for the top of the finished piece and one for the bottom. Cut one long strip 9 inches wide by 60 inches long to be used for the sides. Cut three pieces of fabric, two 21 inches in diameter and one 11 inches wide by 62 inches long. Cover one side of one of the cardboard circles for the top of the hassock and one side of the other circle for the bottom. Then cover one side of the long strip. Turning 1 inch of the fabric under on all sides of all the pieces, pull it very taut and secure it firmly in place with masking tape. Join the two short ends of the long hairpin-lace strip now, securing them along the inside with more masking tape; then sew the fabric edges together along these two short ends. Place the bottom circle in position now, covered side out, and sew it firmly to the side edges. Then sew the lace strip onto the sides, sewing it at top and bottom and sewing only through the spines and hdc sts. Stuff the piece very firmly and then sew the remaining circle, covered side out, in place. To finish the piece, cut another circle of the material 21 inches in diameter, lay it over the top of the hassock, and sew it halfway around. Then stuff the space between this piece and the finished top to achieve a convex shape. Join the opening, stretch the circular piece of hairpin lace over this second top, and sew it in place.

34
. . . And for Indoor Sports

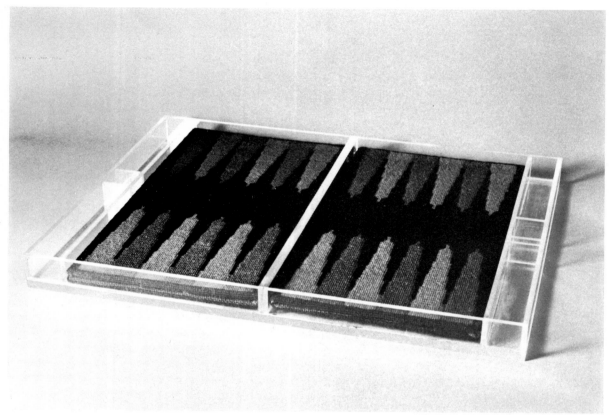

Some like to play backgammon while others prefer chess or checkers. This versatile needlepointed game board is a handsome showpiece that will please all because it is reversible. On one side, in sporty colors of black, red, and green, is the backgammon board. Turn it over, and you're all set for a game of chess or checkers. The board, for which instructions are given here, is assembled into two separate reversible pieces designed to fit into the Plexiglas case we had built for it. Instructions are also given, however, for making just one reversible piece to be hung on the wall when not being used or framed to serve as a tabletop.

Materials:

93 skeins (12 yards each) Red Heart Persian Type needlepoint and crewel
   yarn: 49 skeins in black, 36 skeins in red, and 8 skeins in green
4 pieces needlepoint canvas, 10 mesh to an inch, each 12 × 20¼ inches if
   the board is to be made in two reversible parts (as ours was) or 2 pieces
   each 24 x 20¼ inches if the board is to be made in one piece
masking tape
tapestry needle: #18

The Backgammon Board

Tape the edges of the canvas all around with masking tape to prevent fraying. For the four-part board, start at the lower right corner. Leaving 15 mesh
free at each side and at the top and bottom, follow the color and stitch key
from A to B and rep this pat 2 times more. When this portion of the design
is completed, fill in 5 of the 15 border sts on each of the four sides with the
background color, indicated by a □ on the chart, and leave the remainder
of the canvas free for a turn-under hem after the piece has been finished. To
complete this part of the two-sectioned board, make another piece in exactly
the same manner on a second piece of canvas. For the two-part board, work
the backgammon design in the same manner as above, this time repeating
the color and stitch key from A to B 5 times more on one of the 24- by 20½-
inch pieces of canvas, filling in 5 of the 15 border sts on each of the four
sides with the background color and stitch.

The Checkerboard

For the four-part board, start at the lower right corner. Leaving 21 mesh free
at the starting side, 12 at the opposite side edge, and 18 at the top and bottom, follow the color and stitch key from A to B. Rep this pattern once more
and then rep from A to C 3 times more; complete this sequence of squares
as established across this half of the board. Then work 11 mesh of the outside border, 8 of the top and bottom borders, and 2 of the inside border, in
the color and stitch key as indicated, leaving the remainder of the canvas
free for a turn-under hem. To complete this part of the two-sectioned board,
make another piece in the same manner on a second piece of canvas but
reversing the positions of the inside and outside borders. For the two-part
board, work the checkerboard design in the same manner as above, repeating the color and stitch key from A to B 3 times more, then from A to C 3
times more, and complete this sequence of squares as established across
the remainder of the board. Finish the outside borders as for the two-part
board, eliminating the two inside border sts.

Finishing: Block the finished pieces, turn the unworked edges on all sides
to the wrong side of the work, and tack them in place. For our four separate
pieces, we glued each of the two backgammon pieces onto a piece of cardboard and then glued each of the two parts of the checkerboard onto the reverse side of the cardboard. We then had the special Plexiglas case (see
diagram) constructed to fit the two reversible boards—it has a divider, openings at either end for the playing pieces, and two separate covers with
knobs, one to fit over each board for protection and to heighten its interest
as a showpiece. If just one reversible board has been made, the two pieces
should be sewn to each other, back to back, and then framed between two
panels of glass, clear plastic, or Lucite.

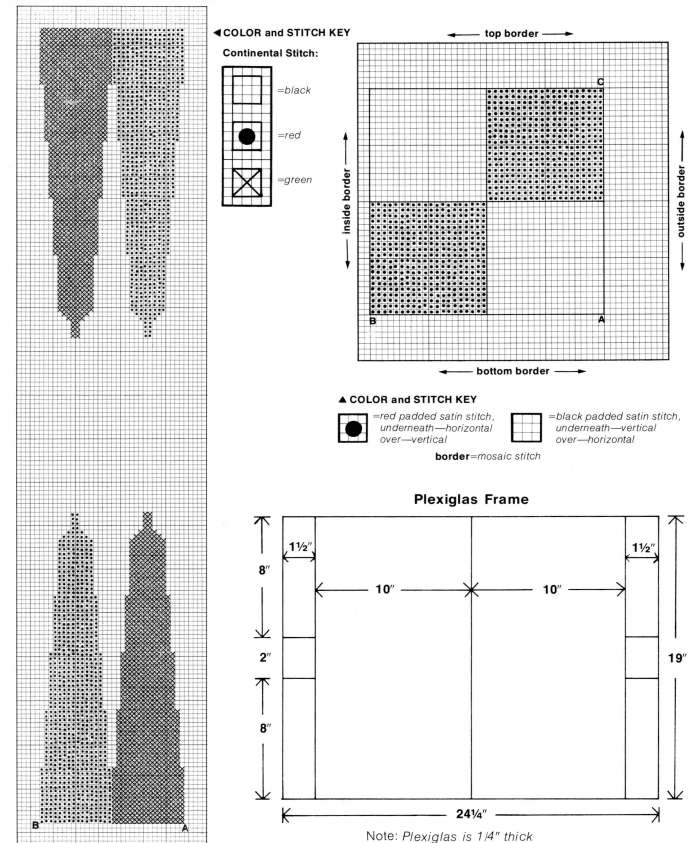

Backgammon board

Checkerboard

◄COLOR and STITCH KEY

Continental Stitch:

=black

=red

=green

top border

inside border

outside border

bottom border

▲ COLOR and STITCH KEY

=red padded satin stitch,
underneath—horizontal
over—vertical

=black padded satin stitch,
underneath—vertical
over—horizontal

border=mosaic stitch

Plexiglas Frame

1½"

8"

2"

8"

10"

10"

1½"

19"

24¼"

Note: *Plexiglas is 1/4" thick*

From left to right: *Oriental Wall Hanging, p. 115;
The Large, Shaggy Pillow, p. 113; Geometric
Textured Rug, p. 110; . . . And for Indoor Sports,
p. 106; An Unusual Hassock, p. 104.*

35
Geometric Textured Rug

The geometric throw rug measures 24 inches by 36 inches. Its tone-on-tone texture and attractive design will complement most decorating schemes, so that the rug can be placed in nearly any room of the house, including the bath. You can complete this versatile and decorative rug—a combination of gros point and latchet-hook work—in about a day with the help of the easy-to-follow chart.

Materials:

7 skeins (3.6 ounces each) Reynolds Lopi in off-white #54
rug canvas, 7 spaces to 2 inches, 26 × 38 inches
masking tape
blunt-ended embroidery needle with a very large eye
latchet hook
3¼ yards self-adhesive rug binding, 1 inch wide

The Rug

Bind all four edges of the rug canvas with masking tape to prevent fraying. With double strands of yarn and the continental stitch, follow the chart to work the gros point portion of the rug. Be sure to center your work so that you have a 1-inch border all around the piece for trimming and hemming later. When the gros point portion of the work has been completed, cut a number of 3-inch lengths of yarn. Using the latchet hook, knot one strand in each space indicated on the chart.

Finishing: Turn the unworked canvas borders to the wrong side of the finished piece and hem them in place, mitering the four corners so that the work lies flat. Then secure the hems more firmly by covering them with rug binding.

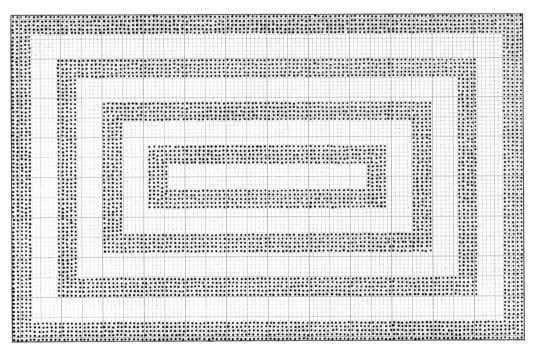

STITCH KEY

=latchet hook   =gros point

From left to right: *Four Glass Jackets, p. 119; For Your Game Table, p. 117; A Pair of Floral Pillows, p. 121.*

36
The Large, Shaggy Pillow

The shaggy floor pillow, a 22-inch square, will be a welcome addition to your living room or den. Its warm ombre shades of brown, rust, and gold will please the eye, and the pillow itself will provide hours of sitting comfort. Following the basic instructions for latchet hooking, you'll work up this pillow in no time at all. Note that each strand of the rya yarn consists of three different-colored strands (brown, rust, and gold) banded together as one. When hooking with this yarn, which is heavier than most, you should work only on every other row to compensate for its weight; if a substitute yarn is used, it must also be worked with three strands at one time.

Materials:

21 bags (1¼ ounces each) Spinnerin precut Real Rya Yarn in shades of
    brown, rust, and gold #655
rug canvas, 7 spaces to 2 inches, 24 × 24 inches
masking tape
latchet hook
1 yard medium- to heavy-weight fabric, 48 inches wide, in rust
heavy-duty thread
2 bags (1 pound each) Poly-Fil or other stuffing material
embroidery needle, approximately 2½ to 3 inches long
2 Prims "Cover-Your-Own"® buttons, each 2½ inches in diameter (size 100)

The Pillow

Bind all four edges of the rug canvas with masking tape to prevent fraying.
Following basic instructions for latchet-hook work, knot one triple strand of
yarn in each space along every other row of the canvas, leaving 1 inch unworked on each of the four sides for trimming and hemming and a square
of 12 spaces free in the center of the piece. When this piece is finished, turn
the unworked edges to the underside and hem them in place. Form the
shape of the pillow by cutting two squares of material, each measuring 23
inches. Turn under ½ inch all around each square and hem in place. With
right sides out and using heavy-duty thread, sew the two pieces together
along three sides; then sew the latchet-hooked work on what will now become
the top of the pillow, sewing it along the four sides of the material. Stuff the
furthermost part of this joined piece very firmly, stuffing 9 inches of the way
in toward the center. Now cover the two button molds with more of the fabric
and sew one over the unworked square in the center of the latchet-hooked
portion of the work. Then, with needle and thread still attached, sew through
to the center of the bottom of the pillow, drawing the thread through very
tightly and securing it very firmly on the other side, thus forming the indenta-
tion in the center of the pillow. Complete stuffing the pillow now, stuffing
around the indented center part, and then sew the edges together along the
fourth side. To complete the pillow, sew the remaining covered button on the
underside of the pillow to cover the stitches that were made to connect the
top button to the bottom of the pillow.

37
Oriental Wall Hanging

The Oriental hanging will dramatize almost any wall in your home. Made in rich colors of garnet, royal blue, empire gold, and rust, this hanging is detailed in design, yet easy to create. Using the basic instructions for latchet hooking, just follow the color key to completion. And, if bare walls aren't a problem in your home, the wall hanging will serve just as well as a hearth rug.

Materials:

30 packs (500 pieces each) Bernat rug wool: 14 packs in cream, 6 packs in garnet, 5 packs in royal, 3 packs in empire gold, and 2 packs in rust
rug canvas, 7 spaces to 2 inches, 21 × 28 inches
masking tape
latchet hook
2 metal rods, each 19 inches long, and a 25-inch metal chain for hanging, or any other desired hanging device or frame

The Hanging

Bind all four edges of the rug canvas with masking tape to prevent fraying. Following basic instructions for latchet-hook work and allowing 1½ inches free on each of the four sides of the canvas for trimming and hemming, follow the color key for the design to completion.

Finishing: Trim the cut yarn ends evenly. Turn 1 inch of the unworked canvas to the wrong side of the piece, trimming away any excess, and hem it in place along the two long edges; then hem the top and bottom edges in place, sewing along the width only and leaving the four 1-inch-wide short edges open. Cover the sewn seams with masking tape. Insert one rod through each of the top and bottom hem openings and attach the piece at the top to the length of metal chain for hanging.

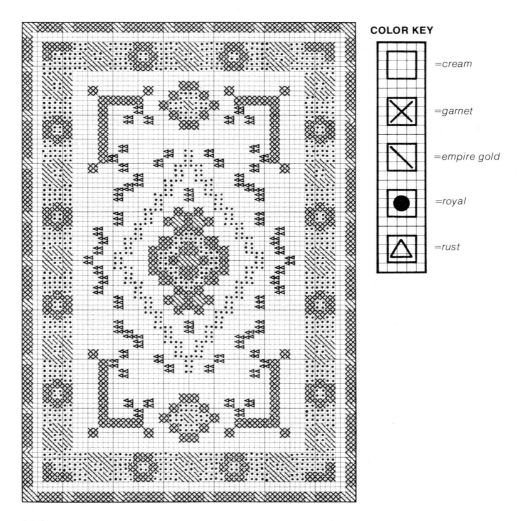

COLOR KEY

□ =cream

⊠ =garnet

◹ =empire gold

● =royal

△ =rust

38
For Your Game Table

The padded cover, lined with white quilted material, will certainly set off your bridge table from all others. It is trimmed in strips of hairpin lace with a center hairpin-lace insert, making it different from most. The top, measuring 30 inches square, is made from plush suede cloth for a bit of elegance—but you can also use plastic cloth for easy care and cleaning. Whether in plastic or suede, this hairpin-lace cover will enhance both your table and your game! And, it's a great gift-giving item, too.

Materials:
2 skeins (2 ounces each) Columbia-Minerva Nantuk sports yarn in larkspur
adjustable hairpin-lace loom
aluminum crochet hook: size F
1 yard suede cloth, 36 inches wide, in color to match yarn
1 yard quilted lining material, 36 inches wide, in white

The Cover

With the loom adjusted to 3 inches, start the hairpin-lace center of the cover by working two strips, each with 22 lps on each side of the loom. Finish both sides of each strip in the following manner: *Work 1 sc through 2 lps together, ch 2, rep from * across, ch 1, and turn. *Next Row:* Work 1 sc in each sc and 2 sc in each ch-2 lp across. Fasten off. Finish the square by sewing the two strips together lengthwise, using an overcast st. Complete the two unfinished edges as follows: With the right side of the work facing, work 1 sc in the outer edge of the strip, *ch 7, 1 sc in the spine, ch 7, 2 sc along the center seam, rep from * and end with 1 sc in the outer edge of the strip on the other side, ch 1, and turn. *Next Row:* Work 1 sc in each sc and 6 sc in each ch-7 lp across (30 sc). Fasten off. Attach yarn to the right side of the work and work 2 rnds of sc around the entire outer edge of the square, working 3 sc in each corner st as you turn. Now make four strips of the hairpin lace to fit around the top outer edge of the cover, working these four strips with 74 lps on each side and finishing them as you did the small center strips. For the dropped edge, make four more strips, each with 94 lps and finished in the same way.

Assembling: Cut a 25-inch square piece of material. Turn under a ½-inch hem on each of the four sides and, mitering the corners, sew it in place. Then cut out a 6-inch-square piece in the center of the cover and discard it. Slit each corner of the remaining square about ½ inch; then turn under to the wrong side a ½-inch hem on each of the four sides and sew it in place. Insert the center square of hairpin lace under the cutout area and sew it in place, attaching the spines at the side edges. Then crochet a chain to fit around the outer edge of the square under which the lace has been inserted and sew it over the joining seam edge. Work 1 additional row of sc now along one edge only of each of the four 74-lp strips. Then cut four 4½-inch squares from the remaining fabric and hem them to measure 3½ inches square. Pin the hairpin-lace strips in place along the four sides of the cover and the 3½-inch fabric pieces in each corner, inserting the lace edges under the fabric edges; sew all pieces in place, including the two spines in each corner. Then crochet chains to fit over all points of joining; sew them in place. Wrong sides together, pin the 94-lp strips to the 74-lp strips and the small fabric corners, joining the crocheted edges together with a sc and sewing the long strip to the fabric corners, using an overcast st. Finish the edge with a rnd of sc worked from left to right instead of right to left. Complete the bottom edge of the drop with a rnd of sc and then another rnd in reverse. Sew the unjoined corner lace spines together.

Finishing: Line the cover by neatly overcasting a 30-inch-square of quilted material, wrong sides together, to the top of the cover. Then cut four 31-inch strips of the material; join them, right sides together, along their short edges; and overcast them to the edge of the 30-inch square and the bottom of the drop.

39
Four Glass Jackets

Made to fit a set of four drinking glasses, each about 3 inches in circumference, these jackets will add a designer's flair to even your everyday water glasses. They are worked in the always-popular bargello flame stitch, with one row on each glass done in a different color for easy identification. Lined with nonporous waterproof material for easy care, these jackets eliminate the need for coasters, serving both you and your furniture well.

Materials:

2 skeins (40 yards each) Columbia-Minerva Lady Handicraft Needlepoint
  Yarn: 1 skein in blue mist, 1 skein in bluebird blue, and small amounts
  in snow white, royal red, and wine red
4 strips needlepoint canvas, 10 mesh to an inch, each 37 × 91 mesh
masking tape
tapestry needle: #18
sharp-pointed sewing needle
⅜ yard thin plastic or other nonporous waterproof material, 36 inches wide,
  for lining

The Jackets

First Jacket: Bind the edges of the canvas piece with masking tape to prevent fraying. Follow the chart to completion, centering the design on the canvas and leaving 3 rows of mesh unworked at top and bottom and at each
side for trimming and hemming later. When the piece has been completed,
cut from the lining material a circle to measure approximately 2¾ inches in
diameter (for the bottom of the jacket) and a strip to measure exactly the size
of the bargello piece. To finish the jacket, weave the side edges together on
the right side of the work, going back and forth from the first stitch on the
strip to the last. Then cut away the 3 rows of unworked mesh on the top and
bottom and two short ends of the piece. Add the lining now, wrong sides together, and with needle and thread sew the side edges together. Then sew
the lining to the top and bottom of the piece. Sew the bottom lining in place
now, right side out, and then, working with the blue mist yarn, embroider a
small cross stitch along the outside of the top and bottom joinings. Make the
remaining jackets in the same manner, substituting a different color for the
royal red on each of the others—snow white on one, wine red on another, and
a second row of blue mist on the third.

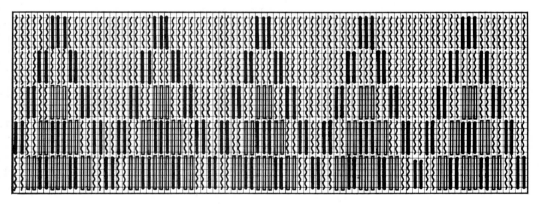

COLOR KEY

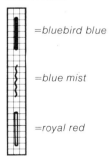

=bluebird blue

=blue mist

=royal red

40
A Pair of Floral Pillows

Delicate in design, these lovely floral pillows will grace any room. The small pillow, a 7½-inch square, and the large one, a 7½- by 13-inch rectangle, are both edged with a charming crocheted chain. The flower pattern is worked in the continental stitch, and the gobelin stitch is used for the quick-to-fill-in background. The back lining for both pillows, which should be a luxurious, soft velvet or suede, adds the finishing touch.

Materials:

7 skeins (40 yards each) Columbia-Minerva Lady Handicraft Needlepoint
Yarn: 3 skeins in snow white, 1 skein each in bluebird blue, blue mist,
olive, and avocado, and small amounts of royal red and wine red
1 skein (2 ounces) Columbia-Minerva Nantuk sports yarn in larkspur, for the
crocheted edges
2 pieces needlepoint canvas, 10 mesh to an inch: one piece 9½ inches
square and one piece 9½ × 15 inches
masking tape
aluminum crochet hook: size G
enough velvet or suede cloth to fit across the back of each pillow
tapestry needle: #18
enough Dacron batting or other material to stuff both pillows

The Large Pillow

Bind the edges of both pieces of canvas with masking tape. Work the double
flower pattern design in the center of the 9½- by 15-inch canvas, following
the color key and working in the continental stitch. When this part of the work
has been completed, fill in the background, leaving a 10-mesh-wide unworked border on each of the four sides for hemming and working in snow
white with the gobelin stitch. Starting at the bottom right-hand corner and
working up toward the top, work each gobelin stitch in the first row over 4
mesh. Starting at the bottom again, work the 1st st of the next row over 2
mesh, the balance of the row over 4 to within the last 2 mesh, and the last
stitch over these 2. Alternate these 2 rows throughout for the pattern, filling
in any irregular number of mesh that occur in the direct area of the center
flower design with the same gobelin stitch, but working it over the required
number of mesh. Complete this portion of the work by turning under to the
wrong side the 1 inch of unworked canvas and hemming it in place.

Crocheted Edging: Using the sport yarn, make a chain long enough to measure 1 inch less than the distance around the four sides of the pillow. Chain
11 more sts and work 1 sc in the 10th ch from the hook, *ch 7, sk 2 ch, sc
in the next ch, rep from * to the end, having 13 ch lps to measure across
each long end of the pillow, 6 across each short end, and 1 additional ch
lp for each of the four corners (42 lps in all). *Rnd 2:* Continuing around, *work
7 sc in the 1st ch lp, sl st in the next sc, rep from * around, and end with
a sl st in the first sc. *Rnd 3:* Ch 5, sk 3 sc of the next lp, sc in the next sc
(ch 5, sc in the 4th sc of the next 7-sc lp) 13 times, [ch 5, sk 2 sc of the next
lp, sc in the next sc, ch 5, sk 2 sc, sc in the next sc]—corner made—(ch 5,
sc in the 4th sc of the next 7-sc group) 6 times; rep between [ ]'s to form the
next corner and complete the remaining two sides and the third corner to
correspond to the first two sides and corners having 14 lps along each long
side and 7 lps along each short side with one additional lp for each corner.
To end the rnd and complete the fourth corner, ch 5 and join with a sl st in
the 1st ch of the starting ch-5. *Rnd 4:* Rep Rnd 2. *Rnd 5:* Rep Rnd 3, increasing 1 lp in each corner in the same manner and having 15 lps along each
long side and 8 lps along each short side of this rnd. *Rnd 6:* Rep Rnd 2. *Rnd
7:* Rep Rnd 3, having 16 lps along each long side and 9 lps along each short
side on this rnd. Work Rnd 2 once more; then fasten off. Sew this edging to
the pillow, sewing the foundation chain on the wrong side of the canvas, just
within the edge, and letting the chain lps extend beyond the edge.

Finishing: Fit the lining material across the back of the pillow and sew it in
place, attaching it to the foundation chain on the wrong side of the work and

sewing it along three sides only. Stuff the pillow firmly and then complete the stitching of the fourth side.

The Small Pillow

Work the single flower pattern design in the center of the 9½-inch-square canvas, following the color key for this pillow. Again, use the continental stitch for the floral portion and the snow white gobelin stitch for the background, as for the large pillow, leaving a 10-mesh-wide unworked border on each side. Work just the 1st and 2nd rnds of the crocheted edging now, having 9 lps on each of the first three sides and 8 lps on the last side. Finish the pillow in the same manner as for the large pillow.

Large Pillow

COLOR and STITCH KEY

Continental Stitch:

△ =snow white

● =blue mist

✕ =bluebird blue

∨ =olive

＼ =avocado

＋ =royal red

－ =wine red

Gobelin Stitch:

☐ =snow white

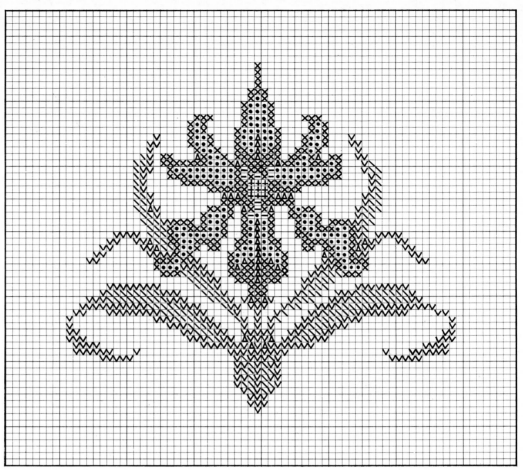

Small Pillow

6

the needlework boutique

The Sporting Scene

41
Deerstalker's Cap

For those crisp autumn mornings, make him this warm, comfortable deerstalker's cap. Complete with visor and ear flaps, the crocheted cap is quite handsome, and bright enough to be spotted by fellow hunters. Worked in classic colors of scarlet and black, the cap is very easy to make—you can complete it in less than half a day! This striking cap is a fine Christmas gift—one that he'll especially appreciate during the blustery winter months.

Materials:
5 skeins (2 ounces each) Reynolds Bulky-Reynelle: 4 skeins in scarlet (MC) and 1 skein in black (CC)
aluminum crochet hook: size K
12 inches of a narrow-gauge, flexible wire

Gauge in Single Crochet: 5 stitches = 2 inches, using double strands of yarn

The Cap

Starting at the top with MC and double strands of yarn, ch 4 and join with a sl st to form a ring. *Next Rnd:* Work 6 sc in the center of the ring. *Next Rnd:* Work 2 sc in each sc around (12 sc). Add a marker to denote start of next and all following rnds. *Next Rnd:* *Sc in the first sc, 2 sc in the next sc, rep from * around (18 sc). *Next Rnd:* *Sc in each of the next 2 sc, 2 sc in the next sc, rep from * around (24 sc). Continue in this manner to inc 6 sts evenly spaced on each rnd, allowing on each 1 st more between points of increase until there are 48 sts in all. Work even on 48 sts until piece measures 8 inches in all, measuring straight down from the top. Then fasten off.

Finishing: With right side of work facing, attach MC to any bottom stitch and work the first ear flap as follows: Sc across 10 sts, ch 1, and turn. Working back and forth on these sts, work even for 4 rows. Then dec 1 st at beg and end of the next row; rep this dec on each of the next 2 rows. When 4 sts remain, fasten off. Skip 2 sts along the base of the hat, attach yarn in the next st, and start the visor: Sc across the next 16 sts, ch 1, and turn. Working back and forth on these sts, work even for 3 rows. Then dec 1 st at beg and end of the next row; rep this dec on each of the next 3 rows. When 8 sts remain, fasten off. Skip the next 2 sts, attach yarn in the next st, and work the second ear flap to correspond to the first. Complete the piece by working 1 rnd of MC sc around the entire bottom of the cap (including the ear flaps and visor), making sure that the work lies flat and rounding out all corners. Fasten off MC, attach CC, and work 1 sc in each sc around, working it around the visor over the strip of wire, bent and shaped to fit the outer contour of the visor. Finally, with right side of work facing, attach double strands of CC to the bottom center of one ear flap to make a tie. Ch 40 and fasten off. Make another tie in the same way at the bottom of the other ear flap.

42
Golf Club Covers

These four gaily colored club covers will add cheer and zest to his golf bag. In a vivid plaid of lemon, skipper blue, paddy green, and white, these knitted covers are both sporty and protective. And more important, each cover is clearly marked with large pieces of bright red ball fringe for easy club identification. Joined with a navy chain, this set will be a welcome gift for anyone who plays golf.

Materials:
2 skeins (4 ounces each) Coats & Clark's Red Heart Fabulend Knitting Worsted in navy and small amounts of white, lemon, skipper blue, and paddy green
2 pairs straight knitting needles: #7 and #10
aluminum crochet hook: size G
2½ yards elastic thread
10 pieces of bright red ball fringe, each ball approximately 1¼ inches in diameter

Gauge in Stockinette Stitch: 4 sts = 1 inch on #10 needles

The Covers

Make four covers: With navy and #10 needles, cast on 38 sts. K 1, p 1 in ribbing for 4½ inches. Change to #7 needles and purl the next row, working 2 sts tog across the row (19 sts). K 1, p 1 in ribbing on these sts for 3 rows. Purl the next row and inc 1 st in each st across the row (38 sts). Working in stockinette st with #10 needles, start the pat and follow the color key to completion. Then shape the top: Working with navy only, p 1 row and then k 2 tog across the next row. Rep these 2 rows once more, ending the last row with k 2 tog, k 1. Break off yarn, leaving a 24-inch thread, and draw the thread tightly through the remaining 10 sts; use the remainder to sew the back seam.

Finishing: Turn the piece to the wrong side and draw elastic thread tightly through each of the 3 rows of k 1, p 1 ribbing made on the #7 needles. Then, right sides out again, trim the plaid portion of the covers with the pieces of ball fringe, as shown in the photograph. To make the connecting chain, attach double strands of navy to any cover, *crochet a 5-inch chain, and attach it to another cover with a sl st. Rep from * until all four covers have been connected with the chain. Fasten off.

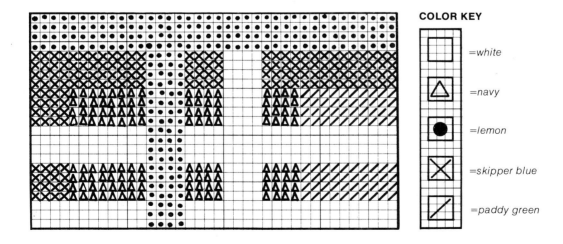

COLOR KEY

☐ =white

△ =navy

● =lemon

⊠ =skipper blue

⧄ =paddy green

Above, from left to right: *Shoestring
Espadrilles, p. 135; After-Swim Cap and
Matching Beach Bag, p. 132.* Right:
Deerstalker's Cap, p. 126.

130

Golf Club Covers, p. 128.

43
After-Swim Cap
and Matching Beach Bag

Whether you make them for yourself or as a gift for someone, the matching beach bag and triangle after-swim scarf are gay leisure accessories that will make a splash on any beach. Their practicality will make them appreciated, too—the scarf covers a wet head attractively while it protects the hair from the damaging rays of a strong sun, and the beach bag can be lined with plastic material so that it can be used to tote around wet bathing gear. Thick, absorbent terry cloth is the base fabric, and hairpin-lace motifs plus crochet form the delicate-looking but sturdy trim. The natural shade of thread contrasts beautifully with any shade of terry cloth, so that you can repeat your swimsuit color in your accessories.

Materials:

8 balls (1 ounce each) Bernat Carioca in natural
adjustable hairpin-lace loom
aluminum crochet hook: size G
1½ yards terry cloth, 36 inches wide, in medium pink
1 yard thin plastic material, 36 inches wide, for waterproof lining (optional)

The Cap

Small Motifs (Make eight): With the loom adjusted to 1 inch, work 14 lps on each side of the spine and fasten off. Finish one side of the inner edge of the motif by working the 14 lps tog with 1 sl st; fasten off and sew the ends of the spine tog. To finish the outer edge, *work 2 lps tog with a sc, ch 7, rep from * around, and end by working a sl st in the 1st sc. Do not fasten off, but continuing around the piece, ch 1 and then work a 2nd row as follows: (Sc and ch 3) 3 times in each ch lp; join the rnd with a sl st in the 1st sc. Fasten off.

Large Motifs (Make three): Adjusting the loom to 2 inches, work 42 lps on each side of the spine and fasten off. To finish one side for the inner edge, *work 6 lps together with 1 sl st, ch 1, rep from * around, and join with a sl st in the 1st sl st. Fasten off and sew the ends of the spine together. On the outer edge, *work 3 lps together with a sc, ch 9, rep from * around, and end by working a sl st in the 1st sc. Do not fasten off, but continuing around the piece, ch 1 and then work a 2nd row as follows: (Sc and ch 3) 3 times in each ch lp; join the rnd with a sl st in the 1st sc and fasten off.

Finishing: To assemble the piece, cut a 19½-inch square of the terry cloth and fold it in half to make a triangle. On top of the folded triangle, arrange the motifs as shown in the diagram. Leave a ¾-inch margin all around the

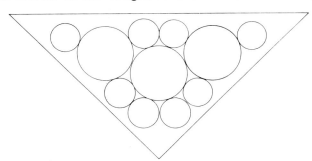

outside edge of the triangle and make sure that the edges of the motifs touch each other when stretched and pinned into place. Sew the motifs in place as pinned, sewing through just one thickness of the triangle. Then fold the ¾-inch allowance along the two side edges to the underside, fold the same edges of the untrimmed piece also to the underside, and sew them together. Trim the side edges of the cap as follows: Ch 160 and, working on 159 sts, work 1 sc in each of the first 79 ch, 3 sc in the center chain (for the apex of the triangle), and 1 sc in each of the remaining 79 ch, ch 1, and turn. Work 3 more rows of sc on these sts, working 1 st in each st and 3 in the center point. Then work a 5th row as follows: *Work 1 sc in each of the first 2 sc, ch 2, sl st in the last sc made, and rep from * around the piece. Fasten off. Sew this piece in position on the cap. Make another 5-row strip for the front of the cap and ties, making this one as a straight piece (without shaping) on 184 sts. When finished, sew it in place, centering it along the front edge of the cap and leaving 32 sts free on each side for tying.

The Beach Bag

Make ten small and four large motifs for each side of the bag, making the motifs in the same manner as those on the cap. To assemble this piece, cut two pieces of the terry cloth, each 18 by 35 inches. One of these pieces is to be used as the lining for the bag; the other is to be trimmed in the following way: Fold the piece in half lengthwise. Leaving a ¾-inch margin free all around, arrange and pin four large and ten small motifs to the top portion of the folded piece, as shown in the diagram. Now sew all the motifs in place.

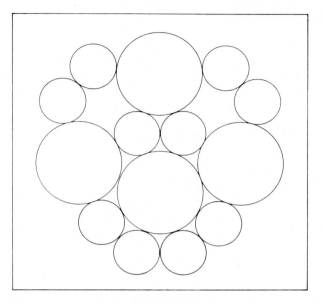

Open the piece at the center fold and trim the remaining outside piece of the bag to correspond to the first side. Pin the untrimmed piece of material as a lining to the underside of the trimmed piece. Leaving ½ inch free for hemming on the top and two sides (the bottom edge remains folded and uncut), round out the shape of the bag as shown, cutting it so that the piece remains 18 inches at the widest measurement, 7½ inches along the folded straight portion, and 10 inches along the straight top opening. Hem each piece now and then sew the lining to the outside portions of the bag. If desired, make the bag waterproof by sewing a piece of thin plastic material over each inside lining piece of the bag.

Finishing: Crochet a length of chain to fit around the bottom and two sides of the bag. Work 2 rows of sc on this chain. Then work 1 row of sc through the back lps only and, finally, 1 more row of sc in the usual manner. Fasten off. Sew this strip in place around three sides of the bag, folding it over on the 3rd row where sts were worked through the back lps only. Make two more chains, each 10 inches long to fit across the two top openings of the bag. Complete these two pieces as you did the one to trim the sides and bottom of the bag. Sew one chain to either side of the top opening, folding them over both the lining and the trimmed portions of the bag. Make the carrying strap for the bag by crocheting a chain 21 inches long, using four strands of yarn together. Sew one end of the chain to each top corner of the bag.

44
Shoestring Espadrilles

Footloose and fancy-free is what these sandals are all about. The fit is perfect because you custom-make them on your own feet with easy macramé work. The straps gracefully cross over your instep and twine around your ankle in a pretty symmetrical pattern. Wooden beads—or pick colorful painted ones to match your sportswear—add a note of interest. The neutral twine shade blends well with all outfits, but be sure to select a soft, cottony twine for the most comfortable wear.

Materials:

66 yards heavy-duty wrapping twine, 60-pound test

1 piece of inner-sole leather and 1 piece sole leather, each approximately 2 inches longer and wider than the contour of the soles of your right and left feet

awl

4 large-holed, round wooden beads, each approximately 1 inch in diameter

Duco cement or other nonsoluble glue

sharp knife for leather cutting

embroidery needle with a very large eye

The Sandals

Preparation: Outline the right foot, rounding out the toes, onto the piece of sole leather and cut out the traced portion, leaving a 1-inch allowance all around. Cut another piece, to correspond, for the left foot. Then cut two pieces in the same manner from the inner-sole leather. Working on the inner-sole leather piece for the right foot now and following the diagram, draw the outline of your toes and mark the point of division between each toe (points 1 through 4 on the diagram). Make another mark (point 5) just above the bunion bone on your foot, another just in front of the ankle bone (point 6), and seventh and eighth ones directly across from the fifth and sixth ones on the opposite side of the sole. Punch a large hole with the awl through each of the eight marks on this piece of leather. Now cut ten 3¼-yard strands of the twine. Thread one strand into the needle and draw it through points 1 and 2 on the chart, inserting the needle from the right to the wrong side at point 1 and drawing it out at point 2, pulling both ends of the twine to an even length. Draw one more strand through these two holes. In the same manner, draw two lengths of twine through points 3 and 4, two through points 5 and 6, two through 7 and 8, and two additional ones through points 6 and 8 (there are now four strands drawn through these last two points). Now center the bottom of the strung inner sole on the wrong side of the outer sole and glue the two pieces together. When they are firmly set in position, cut away the margins from the actual foot tracing and begin to macramé.

Macramé: With the sole placed under your foot to achieve a perfect fit and remembering that all square knots for the right foot are made from left to right and all those for the left foot are worked from right to left, work as follows: *Row 1:* Make a square knot over the second toe with strands coming through points 1 and 2 and another over the fourth toe with strands coming through points 3 and 4. *Row 2:* With center four strands, make a square knot over the third toe slightly above (higher on the instep) the two on Row 1, using your own foot as a spacing guide. *Row 3:* With the two left outside strands of the center knot and two strands from point 5, make a square knot directly above point 5 and the first knot on Row 1; make another knot to correspond, using the two right outside strands of the center knot and the two strands from point 7. Thread the four center strands now through one bead; then draw through that same bead the innermost strand of each group of four to the right and left of the center. The bead is now threaded onto six strands of the twine. *Row 4:* With the three outer strands on the left side and one strand closest to these from the center beaded group, make a square knot directly above the first knot on Row 3; make another knot to correspond on the right side of the sandal. Then make a third square knot on this row with the four remaining strands, this one directly above the bead. *Row 5:* Drop the two outermost strands on each side of the foot and, with the remaining eight center strands, make two square knots, placing one on either side of the knot on Row 4. *Row*

6: Drop the two outermost strands of the two knots made on Row 5 and, with the remaining four free strands, make one center square knot, directly between but above the two knots on Row 5. At this point, draw the center six strands through a second bead and then go on to repeat Rows 4, 5, and 6. Start the strap portion now and work in the following manner: *With the two strands at point 6 closest to the toe end of the sole and the two outer strands of the left knot on the previous row, make one square knot, using your foot as a guide for its placement. Make another knot in the same manner on the right side of the shoe at point 8. Now with the two strands closest to the ankle at point 6 and two adjacent strands from the previous knot, make another knot just above the last knot next to the first one on that side; repeat on the right side of the shoe. Divide the strands into two groups of ten each now and cross them over the top of your foot, just in front of the ankle (in the way you will be wearing them). Working with the straps in this position for proper spacing and being sure to keep the group of ten strands that you will be working on for one strap straight and even, *leave 2 inches of free space and make one square knot with the outer group of four strands, leaving the two center strands free. Make another knot with the inner group of four strands. The shortest free strand before this knot should measure approximately 1¼ inches. Now make a square knot using the two free center strands and one adjacent one on each side from the previous two knots just made. Complete this portion of the design with two more knots on either side of the center one just made. Then leave 1¼ inches of free space* and rep from between *'s 4 times, or for the number of times desired for the wraparound strap. Complete the left strap to correspond to the right one, wrap the straps around your leg, and tie the ends at the back in a large square knot. Cut away any excess lengths at this point, leaving 2 or 3 inches free after the knot has been made and trimming the ends evenly. Make a slip knot at the end of each free-hanging strand. Work the left shoe to correspond to the right one, just completed.

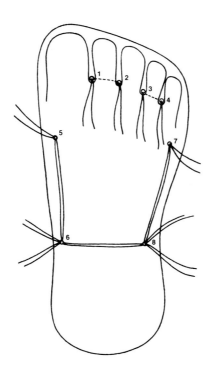

45
A Tennis Cap and Racket Cover

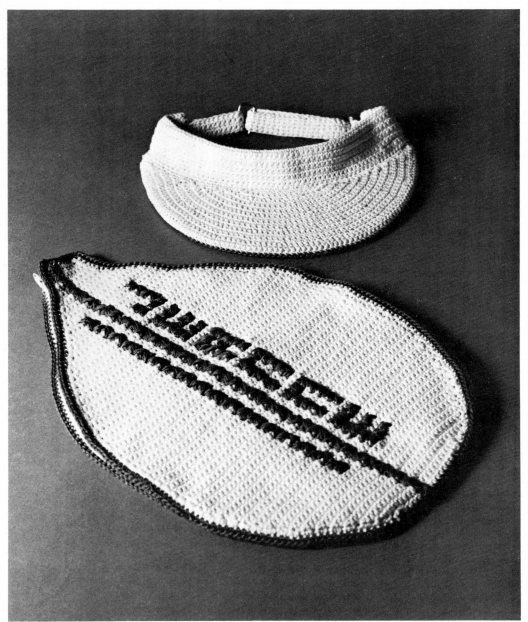

The woman who sports this attractive crocheted tennis visor and racket cover can't lose. Smartly styled and made with an adjustable buckle, the visor will fit any size head. The racket cover, the charming complement of the cap, is personalized with the player's name. In crisp white and bright green, it will be a smash on any tennis court.

Materials:

8 balls Coats & Clark's "Speed-Cro-Sheen": 6 balls in white (MC) and 2 balls in bright green (CC)

aluminum crochet hook: size E

1 1¼-inch adjustable buckle, a 1¼-inch slide buckle, and a 10-inch square of cardboard for the cap, and a 12-inch zipper for the cover

embroidery needle with a large eye

Gauge in Single Crochet: 5 stitches = 1 inch; 6 rows = 1 inch

The Cap

Visor: Starting at the outside edge, ch 85 with MC. Working in sc throughout, work 1 row even on 84 sts. Then work as follows: *Row 1:* *Sc across 5 sts, work 2 tog, rep from * 11 times, ch 1, and turn (72 sts). *Rows 2,3, and 4:* Dec 1 st at beg and end of each row (66 sts). *Row 5:* *Sc across 4 sts, work 2 tog, rep from * 10 times, ch 1, and turn (55 sts). *Rows 6,7,8,9, and 10:* Dec 1 at beg and end of each row (45 sts). *Row 11:* *Sc across 3 sts, work 2 tog, rep from * 8 times, ch 1, and turn (36 sts). *Row 12:* *Sc across 4 sts, work 2 tog, rep from * 5 times, ch 1, and turn (30 sts). *Row 13:* Dec 1 st at beg and end of row (28 sts). *Row 14:* Sl st across the first 4 sts, sc to within the last 4 sts, and fasten off. With CC, make another piece in the same manner for the underside of the visor. With right sides out, sew this piece to the MC piece around the outside curved edge, leaving the top portion open. Cut a piece of cardboard to the size and shape of the visor, insert it between the two partially joined pieces, and then complete the top joining.

Front Band: Starting at the top, ch 75 with MC. Then work in sc on 74 sts for 10 rows. On the next row, sl st across the first 6 sts, work in sc to within the last 6 sts, and fasten off. Work 11 rows in the same manner along the opposite side of the starting chain. Fold the piece in half lengthwise and sew the bottom edges together. Then sew the sc portion of that joined edge to the top of the visor, allowing the joined sl st edges to extend on either side.

Back Straps: With MC, ch 25 for the short strap. Then work even in sc on 24 sts for 5 rows and fasten off. Sew one short end of this strap to the middle of the short end of the front band of the cap, draw the center of it through one side of the slide buckle, and then sew the other short end to the same part of the cap on which the first was sewn. For the longer strap, ch 52 with MC and work in sc on 51 sts for 5 rows. Fasten off. Sew one short end of this strap to the middle of the other short end of the front band, draw it through the other side of the slide buckle, and then draw the other short end for approximately 1 inch through the adjustable buckle; sew it in place.

The Racket Cover

Make two pieces: Starting at the handle opening with MC, ch 9. Work even in sc on 8 sts for 4 rows. Then inc 1 st at beg and end of every row 12 times and at beg and end of every other row 11 times (54 sts). Work even until piece measures 10 inches in all. Then dec 1 st at beg and end of every other row 6 times and every row 11 times (20 sts). Dec 2 sts at beg of next row and work to within the last 2 sts. Fasten off.

Finishing: With MC and right side of work facing, work 1 row of sc around each piece, making sure that the work lies flat, rounding out the bottoms, and working 3 sc in each corner st at the top of each piece. Fasten off MC, attach CC, and work 1 sc in each sc around, again working 3 sc in each top corner st as you turn. Fasten off CC. On what will now become the top side of the racket cover, embroider with triple strands of CC and a cross stitch a straight line down the full length of that piece, working from the top down, starting at the 2nd st from the left at the top edge and working across 1 st and 2 rows for each cross stitch. Leaving a 1-st sp to the right of the line just completed, embroider the desired name or initials, again with triple strands of CC and a cross stitch, following the alphabet chart on page 8 and centering the vertical space that the letters will occupy between the top and bottom of the cover. Allowing a 1-st sp to the left of the embroidered line, embroider, again with triple strands of CC and a cross stitch, a straight line the equivalent length of the embroidered name or monogram. Finally, finish the cover by joining the two pieces, right sides out, with a row of CC sl st, starting at the upper right corner and working to within 12 inches of the upper left corner. Sl st each remaining 12-inch edge separately to allow for the zipper opening. Fasten off, and sew the zipper in place along the 12-inch opening.

A Tennis Cap and Racket Cover, p. 138.

46
For His Skiing,
A Cap and Mittens

For skiing, or for everyday wear, keep him warm in this Scandinavian-style woolen ski cap and mittens. Patterned in the traditional snow-flake motif, this beautiful set is worked in a sky blue and winter white. It is done on a gauge with enough elasticity so that one size fits all. Knit in the simple stockinette stitch, it's easy to make and a perfect gift-giving item for the Christmas season.

Materials:

3 skeins (4 ounces each) Reynolds Reynelle knitting worsted: 2 skeins in co-
lonial (MC) and 1 skein in white (CC)
2 pairs straight knitting needles: #7 and #10
2 stitch holders

Gauge in Stockinette Stitch: 9 stitches = 2 inches; 6 rows = 1 inch

The Cap

Starting at the top with MC and #10 needles, cast on 6 sts. Knit the first row, increasing 1 st in each st to make 12 sts. *Next Row:* Purl. Rep the last 2 rows once to make 24 sts. *Next Row:* *K 1, inc 1 st in the next st, rep from * across to make 36 sts. *Next Row:* Purl. *Next Row:* *K 2, inc 1 in the next st, rep from * across to make 48 sts. *Next Row:* Purl. Continue in this manner, working in stockinette st throughout, to inc 12 sts evenly spaced on every other row, having 1 st more between each point of inc, until there are 72 sts in all. Then work 1 row even. *Next Row:* *K 11, inc 1 st in the next st, rep from * across to make 78 sts. *Next Row:* Purl. *Next Row:* *K 12, inc 1 st in the next st, rep from * across to make 84 sts. *Next Row:* Purl. *Next Row:* *K 13, inc 1 st in the next st, rep from * across to make 90 sts. *Next Row:* Purl, decreasing 1 st at beg of the row (89 sts). Start working the snowflake pat now, following the design chart to the completion of the 15 rows shown. Then, working in MC only, p 1 row and then k 1 row, increasing 1 st at beg of this last row. Change to #7 needles and work in k 1, p 1 ribbing on 90 sts for 6 inches. Bind off loosely in ribbing. Sew back seam.

The Mittens

Right Mitten: With MC and #7 needles, cast on 34 sts. K 1, p 1 in ribbing for 3 inches. Then change to #10 needles and, working in stockinette st throughout, work in MC for 2 rows. Then start pat. Following the design chart to completion, work even for 6 rows and then shape the thumb gusset: *Row 1:* K 17, p 1, place a marker on the needle, k 2, place another marker on the needle, p 1, k 13. *Row 2:* P 13, k 1, p 2, k 1, p 17. *Row 3:* K 17, p 1, inc 1 st in each of the next 2 sts, p 1, k 13. *Row 4:* P 13, k 1, p 4, k 1, p 17. *Row 5:* K 17, p 1, inc 1 in next st, k to 1 st before next marker, inc 1 in next st, p 1, k 13. *Row 6:* P 13, k 1, p to next marker, k 1, p 17. Rep the last 2 rows twice more (42 sts). *Thumb:* On next row, k 17 and sl these sts onto a holder, k next 12 sts, and sl remaining 13 sts onto another holder. Work even now on 12 sts until the thumb measures ½ inch less than the desired finished length, ending with a purl row. To shape the top of the thumb, k 2 tog across the row. Purl the next row. On the next row, k 2 tog across the row. Break off yarn, leaving a 10-inch thread. Draw the thread through the remaining sts, pull up tightly, and then sew the thumb seam with the remainder. *Hand:* With right side of work facing, sl 17 sts from the first holder onto a #10 needle, pick up and k 4 sts across the start of the thumb, and then k the 13 sts from the second holder (34 sts). P 1 row and then work even until piece measures 5¼ inches below the point where all sts were joined after the completion of thumb, ending with a purl row. To shape the top, work as follows: *Row 1:* *K 1, sl 1, k 1, psso, k 11, k 2 tog, k 1*, place a marker on the needle, and rep between *'s once more. *Row 2:* Purl. Continue in this manner to dec 1 st at each end of needle and 1 st at each side of marker every other row twice more and then p 1 row. *Next Row:* Work 2 sts tog across the row. Bind off.

Left Mitten: Work to correspond to the right mitten as far as the start of the thumb gusset. To shape the thumb gusset: K 13, p 1, place a marker on the

Above: *For His Skiing, A Cap and Mittens, p. 142.* Right: *A Young Ballerina's Ice Skating Skirt, p. 146.*

144

needle, k 2, place another marker on the needle, p 1, k 17. Finish this mitten to correspond to the right mitten.

Finishing: Sew both side seams of mittens.

Ski Cap

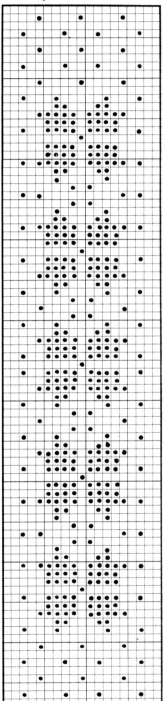

Ski Mitten

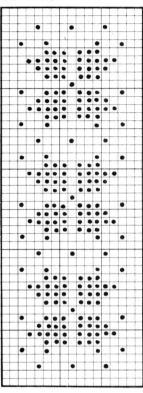

COLOR KEY

 = MC   = CC

47
A Young Ballerina's Ice Skating Skirt

Soft and furry, the young ballerina's ice skating skirt will swirl with every turn she makes. It has a comfortable elastic waist and is trimmed with colorful braids and bows. The directions are written for size 6 with instructions for sizes 8, 10, and 12 provided in parentheses. The size-6 skirt is planned for an approximate length of 11½ inches (12-inch length for size 8, 13-inch length for size 10, and 14-inch length for size 12). If you wish to make the length of the skirt either shorter or longer, do so before the first decrease row.

Materials:
6 (7,8,9) balls (1¾ ounces each) Unger Fluffy: 3 (4,5,6) balls in white (MC)
and 1 ball each in bright red (A), medium blue (B), and navy (C)
straight knitting needles: #7
aluminum crochet hook: size F
enough elastic, ½ inch wide, to fit waist measurement

Gauge in Stockinette Stitch: 9 stitches = 2 inches; 6 rows = 1 inch

The Skirt

Make two pieces: With MC, cast on 243 (252,261,270) sts. Working in pat st throughout, work even for ½ (2,4,6) inch. Then work as follows: *Next Row:* *K 25 (26,27,28), k 2 tog, and rep from * across the row until 234 (243,252,261) sts remain. Work even for 5 rows. *Next Row:* *K 24 (25,26,27), k 2 tog, rep from * across the row until 225 (234,243,252) sts remain. Work 5 rows even. Continue now to dec 9 sts evenly spaced on every 6th row, allowing each time 1 st less between each point of decrease 3 (2,1,0) times more. When 198 (216,234,252) sts remain, work as follows: *Next Row:* *K 9 (10,11,12), k 2 tog, rep from * across the row until 180 (198,216,234) sts remain. Work even for 3 rows. *Next Row:* *K 8 (9,10,11), k 2 tog, rep from * across the row until 162 (180,198,216) sts remain. Work even for 3 rows. *Next Row:* K 7 (8,9,10), k 2 tog, rep from * across the row until 144 (162,180,198) sts remain. Work even for 3 rows. Continue now to dec 18 sts evenly spaced on every 4th row, allowing each time 1 st less between each point of decrease, 5 times more. When 54 (72,90,108) sts remain, work 3 rows even. For size 6, continue to work even until piece measures the desired length and then bind off. For size 8, *k 4, k 2 tog, and rep from * across the row. Then work even on 60 sts for the desired length and bind off. For size 10, *k 3, k 2 tog, rep from * across the row until 72 sts remain; work 1 row even. On the next row, *k 7, k 2 tog, and rep from * across the row. Then work even on 64 sts for the desired length and bind off. For size 12, *k 4, k 2 tog, and rep from * across the row until 90 sts remain; work 1 row even. On the next row, *k 3, k 2 tog, and rep from * across the row. Work even on 72 sts for desired length, bind off, and seam sides. With MC and right side of work facing, work 2 rows of sc around the bottom of the skirt and 4 rows around the waist.

Casing: Turn skirt to the wrong side and work a casing along the 4-row sc waistband border as follows: Attach MC to the top of one side seam of the casing, *ch 3, skip ½ inch, work a sl st at the bottom of the waistband, *ch 3, skip ½ inch, and work a sl st at the top of the waistband; rep from * around the entire piece. Fasten off. Cut elastic to fit the waist measurement, draw it through the casing, and sew the short ends together.

Braided Trim: Make the three bands of braided trim for the bottom of the skirt as follows: for each band, ch 550 sts, using double strands of yarn in each of colors A, B, and C. Then braid the three different-colored chains. Make two more bands in the same way. Sew one of these braided bands on top of the bottom 2 rows of single crochet, cutting away any excess braid when finished. Sew the second braid approximately 1½ inches above the top of the first braid, contouring it to follow the lines of decrease (see the project photograph); cut away any excess braid. Sew the third band approximately ¾ inch above the second one, following the same contour and again cutting away any excess. To make the bows, chain 100 sts with each of colors A,B, and C, again using double yarn. Braid the chains, shape each into a bow, knot the two ends, and sew it into place (see the project photograph).

147

7

the
needlework boutique

A
Guide to Needlework Perfection

On the pages immediately preceding these, we have presented, through illustration and explanation, the "how-to" techniques involved in the making of the various needlework projects shown in this book. Here now, in order to help you create a more perfect piece of work, we offer other important information to guide you in the preparation, the actual working, and the final finishing of whatever it is you have chosen to make.

Certain basic rules apply to all craftwork, such as having all your working tools and materials on hand before you begin. When you buy your materials, you should be selective to the point of knowing that they will be durable and of good enough quality to warrant the amount of work you'll be doing with them; also be sure you've bought a sufficient amount so that you will not run short before having completed your work, thus running the risk of needing to finish with yarn or thread of a different dye lot.

Beyond this, your work should be approached in an easy mood and with the feeling of confidence that you are going to do a fine piece of work. Unfortunately, tension reflects itself in handwork, so that it is not possible to get the smooth, even look you would like to have if you are not relaxed. The instructions given for each project are simple and easy to follow, and you should feel assured that what you are making will be good if you read them carefully, step by step, as you work. A good rule to follow, in this direction, is to read only the first thing you need to know and to do that for the necessary number of inches or rows indicated; then go on to read what needs to be done next.

General Finishing Techniques

Fringing, or putting a final edging around a piece of completed work, is often called for in the finishing process. When instructions specify using "color over color" in this part of the work, you must use the same color yarn as the color that appears in the stitch or stitches just above or alongside whatever finishing work you are doing.

Seaming, too, is often necessary as part of the finishing process. There are three popular methods of seaming: woven seams, sewn seams, and crocheted seams. In all three instances, the pieces to be joined must be matched carefully and the seaming done with the same yarn as that with which the pieces were worked. *Woven seams* are worked with a blunt-ended tapestry needle on the right side of the finished pieces. The needle is inserted through the first stitch on one edge, drawn through two strands along the edge, and then worked through two strands on the opposite side edge. *A sewn seam* is also worked with a blunt-ended tapestry needle and approximately a ¼-inch-long running backstitch on the wrong side of the work. The *crocheted seam* is worked with a fine crochet hook on the wrong side of the work (sometimes on the right side for design effect when so specified in instructions) with either a single crochet or a slip stitch, working together through the thicknesses of the stitches on each side of each of the edges to be joined.

Blocking, the final finish to any piece of work, is also necessary in almost all needlecraft projects and may be done either before or after the pieces are assembled. Unless otherwise instructed, lay the work flat, cover it with a damp cloth, and press it lightly with an iron, allowing steam to form and keeping the iron moving over the piece. Most pieces made with synthetic yarns will have little resiliency to them, so that they will remain close to the size to which they were made; wool pieces, however, and even some cotton can be stretched slightly if desired while the garment is still damp.

For Macramé, Latchet-Hook, and Hairpin-Lace Work

Among the various skills employed in this book, there are two that involve the art of knotting—macramé and latchet-hook work. Both are relatively simple and basically involve only the guide rules given above. Macramé, the art practiced by early seamen who found the making of knots a fascinating way of filling long, empty hours, can be well done with the use of good materials, an even tension, and the careful step-by-step following of instructions. In latchet-hook work, the stitches are outlined and already gauged for you by means of the openings of the woven canvas that serves as the background for this type of work. These openings also help to prevent any uneven tension or irregularity in your work, consequently making the basic rules, given earlier in this chapter, perfectly adequate for completing a fine piece of work in this medium.

The art of making a piece of hairpin lace is also a relatively simple one, again involving strict adherence to the instructions for the particular project being made and an observance of the guide rules above—the purchase of good and sufficient materials, the use of a relaxed, even tension, and the use of a proper finishing technique.

The remaining arts, those of knitting and crochet work and needlepoint and embroidery, are perhaps just a little more involved, so that in doing these, one should be concerned with a few other basic principles of working them correctly. Toward this end we offer the following information.

For Knitting and Crochet Work

Gauge is the key word that spells out the final success or failure of any knitted or crocheted project. In either of these media, it means the number of stitches and rows you are working to an inch. To achieve a perfect fit in any garment, it is most important that the number of stitches you get to each inch of your work (and the number of rows, when specified) are exactly the same as those called for in the instructions. To be certain that your work will measure correctly, it is always necessary that you make a 3- or 4-inch square swatch with the yarn, needles, and stitch you are going to use and then to measure your swatch on a stitch gauge. If you are getting more than the prescribed number of stitches per inch, try larger needles or a larger hook; if you are getting fewer, make another sample piece using smaller needles or a smaller hook. The little extra time you devote to testing your "hand" before starting your actual piece of work will be very well worth the effort made.

Joining Yarn: Joining a new ball of yarn should always be done at the beginning or end of a row, even though the old ball of yarn may run out in the middle of a row and a small length of yarn may need to be wasted. In both knitting and crocheting, the new yarn is attached at the end of the last row that was finished with the old yarn and the next row is started with the new yarn.

Changing Colors: When the change of color occurs in knitting at the start of a new row, simply work the last stitch on the last row with the old color and start the next row with the new. When it occurs, however, somewhere along the row, always bring the new color to be used from under and around the color just dropped so that the yarn is twisted and the work lies smooth and flat. When working in this way, the color not being used must always be carried loosely across the back so that it does not draw together the stitches being worked. In crocheting, when a change of color occurs somewhere along the row, the last stitch of the original color is worked with that color until just two loops of that last stitch remain on the hook. Those two loops are then removed with the new color. When the change occurs at the start of a new row, the last two loops of the last stitch on the row just finished are the ones that are removed with the new color.

Ripping: Sometimes during the course of knitting or crocheting, you will discover an error several rows after it has occurred. The choice is either to rip it out or to overlook it and probably always be aware of it, even though the error may involve only one stitch. If the error is just a dropped stitch in a knitted piece, you can pick it up relatively easily with a crochet hook. To do this, insert the hook into the dropped stitch, *catch the loose strand of yarn on the next row in back of the hook, and pull the loop through on the hook. Repeat from the *, working up each row until the top strand has been pulled through. Then place the last loop on the left needle and continue with your knitting. When ripping is necessary, withdraw the needles from your work, rip to one row below the row in which the error occurred, and then rip out the next row, stitch by stitch, inserting one of the two free needles into each stitch as you go. When all the stitches have been picked up in this way, you can continue with your knitting again.

In crochet work, ripping is an equally painful although much simpler procedure. Since each row is a completed row by itself, there is no need to pick up stitches after having ripped back to where the error has occurred. In this case, having ripped to one stitch before the error, simply insert your hook into that stitch and continue with your crocheting again.

For Embroidery Work

Background Fabric, Needles, and Thread: The choice of the proper background fabric for embroidery work is a very important one, both for the ease of working and for the general appearance of the finished piece. An even, open-weave fabric on which the space produced by the angle of the vertical and horizontal threads is visible is the best type to use, since the threads can be easily counted and, consequently, a greater degree of regularity can be achieved in the actual stitchery. Linen is very often the best choice because its surface is hard enough not to pill or pucker while being worked on and its weight should be heavy enough to accommodate the weight of the embroidery thread so that the threads being drawn through do not distort the fabric itself. The size of the cut material should be at least 1 inch larger on all four sides than the actual piece of finished work, and the four sides should be sealed with masking tape before the work is started in order to prevent any fraying of the edges. Needles should be sharp-ended and of medium length for ease of work;

they should also have long, slender eyes suitable for threading multiple strands, yet shaped so that they will not form a hole in the material when being drawn through. When several colors of thread are being used, it is wise to work with more than one needle to avoid the abrasive wear and tear caused by frequent re-threading.

Enlarging a Design: To enlarge a design for embroidery, trace the design and then transfer it to graph paper, using a sheet of carbon between. Box in the design on the graph paper so that you can count how many squares have been used. Now, draw a box on another piece of paper to the size you wish the finished design to be. Divide this into the same number of squares as the first one; then copy the design, square by square, onto it. To copy a curved line across several squares, mark where it crosses the squares and then join the marks.

Transferring a Design: Although the transferring of a design onto material is a relatively simple procedure, it should be done very carefully—a little patience at this time will ensure a smoother and more accurate design to work with. To make the transfer, place dressmaker's tracing paper, carbon side down, on the right side of the fabric and lay the traced design on top. Then trace over the design with a pencil, being careful to hold the design in place so that the tracing does not become distorted yet holding it lightly enough that the carbon won't smudge the material.

For Needlepoint

Stitching Techniques: Having cut and taped your canvas in the same manner as described for the preparation of the background material for embroidery work, you are ready to start stitching but should be aware of certain techniques before you do. Cut the yarn to be used to a comfortable working length, usually about 18 inches. When threading your needle, do not let the short end of the yarn extend more than 2 or 3 inches beyond the needle eye, for the constant drawing of double yarn through the canvas will cause an uneven tension in the work. When starting with a new strand of yarn, do not knot the end; instead, leave a 2- or 3-inch strand free on the wrong side of the work. Work the first four or five stitches over the free strand in the back and then cut off the remainder. When coming to the end of a piece of yarn, draw your needle through to the underside of the work, turn the canvas over, and, working on the wrong side, weave your needle over and under every other stitch just completed for about 1 inch. Then cut off the remaining end of yarn. To further ensure the neatness of a finished piece of work, avoid possible distortion by working different areas of the canvas rather than proceeding directly from one corner or edge to the opposite one. Also, although a single thrust of the needle from top surface to top surface may be a faster way of working, thrusting it up and down with two separate motions will help to relieve the pull on the mesh of the canvas.

Blocking: It is usually necessary to ease a finished piece of needlepoint back into shape by blocking it, since some amount of distortion will occur during the working process. The simplest way of blocking is to pin the piece right side up on a board, being sure to use rustproof pins and to have the corners absolutely at right angles and the parallel sides stretched to exactly the right length. Dampen the canvas and leave it pinned until it is completely dry; then press it lightly if desired.

Crochet

Foundation Chain

Knot a loop onto the hook. Holding the hook in your right hand and the end of the yarn extending from the loop between the thumb and middle finger of your left hand, loop the yarn to be worked over the index finger of your left hand. The balance of that yarn should extend from the same hand, lightly held in control between the ring and little fingers. Then *pass the hook under the extending yarn nearest to the hook and draw both the hook and the yarn through the loop already on the hook (the first stitch). Repeat from * for as many stitches as the instructions specify. (Note: Turning chains are worked in the same way as are chain stitches indicated in a pattern stitch—the last loop worked is the one through which the yarn and hook of the next stitch are drawn.)

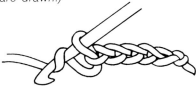

Slip Stitch

Insert the hook through the two upper strands of the stitch to be worked, place the yarn over the hook, and then draw both yarn and the hook through the stitch and through the last loop on the hook.

Single Crochet

Insert the hook through the two upper strands of the stitch to be worked, place the yarn over the hook and draw it through the stitch, then yarn over again and draw it through the remaining two loops on the hook. When working the first row of the single crochet on a foundation chain, start your first stitch in the second chain from the hook and always chain 1 to turn when the first stitch on the next row is to be a single crochet.

Half Double Crochet

Place the yarn over the hook and then insert the hook through the two upper strands of the stitch to be worked. Draw the yarn through the stitch, yarn over again, and draw it through the remaining three loops on the hook. When working the first row of half double crochet on a foundation chain, start your first stitch in the third chain from the hook and always chain 2 to turn when the first stitch on the next row is to be a half double crochet.

Double Crochet

Place the yarn over the hook and then insert the hook through the two upper strands of the stitch to be worked. Draw the yarn through the stitch, yarn over, draw it through two loops on the hook, yarn over again, and draw it through the remaining two loops on the hook. When working the first row of double crochet on a foundation chain, start your first stitch in the third chain from the hook and always chain 2 to turn when the first stitch on the next row is to be a double crochet.

Treble Crochet

Place the yarn twice over the hook and then insert the hook through the two upper strands of the stitch to be worked. Draw the yarn through the stitch, place the yarn over the hook, and draw it through two loops on the hook three times. When working the first row of treble crochet on a foundation chain, start your first stitch in the fourth chain from the hook and always chain 3 to turn when the first stitch on the next row is to be a treble crochet.

Double Treble Crochet

Work as the treble crochet except wrap the yarn three times over the hook instead of twice and take two loops off four times instead of three.

Triple Treble Crochet

Work as the treble crochet except wrap the yarn four times over the hook instead of twice and take two loops off five times instead of three times.

Increasing and Decreasing

When it is necessary to increase in a single crochet stitch, the basic formula is to work 2 stitches in the same stitch, thus forming an extra stitch. The new stitch would also be worked in single crochet, since a new stitch is always worked in the same type of stitch as the original in which the increase is being made. In double crochet, for example, the stitch to be increased would be worked in double crochet, and in treble crochet it would be a treble crochet. To decrease in single crochet, work off 2 stitches as one, thus decreasing, or "losing," a stitch. Do this by drawing up a loop in the next single crochet, then draw up another loop in the following single crochet, wrap the yarn over the hook and draw it through all three loops at once. Again, since the same stitch pattern is always maintained, as in increasing, to decrease a double crochet stitch, work your first double crochet to the point where 2 loops remain on the hook, then yarn over and insert the hook in the next stitch, yarn over and draw through the stitch, yarn over and draw through two loops, yarn over and draw through the remaining three loops.

Hairpin Lace

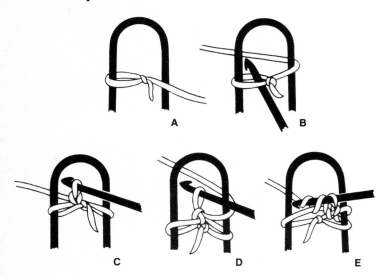

Figure A

Tie a slip knot equal to half the adjusted width of the loom, remove the holding bar at the bottom of the loom, and place the left prong into the loop. Replace the bar.

Figure B

Wind the yarn around the right prong of the loom and across the back of it; then insert a crochet hook between the two strands of the loop to the left of the center of the loom, placing the hook under the front strand.

Figure C

Place the yarn that lies across the back of the loom over the hook and draw it through the loop, reach again for the yarn, place it over the hook, and draw it through the loop on the hook.

Figure D

Remove the hook from the stitch and reinsert it into the same stitch from the back. Turn the loom toward you now, from right to left, thus making a new loop of yarn around the back of the loom.

Figure E

Insert the hook between the two strands of the loop to the left of the center, placing it under the front strand. Then place the yarn that is across the back of the loom over the hook, draw it through, reach again for the yarn, and draw it through both loops on the hook, thus making a single crochet stitch, a series of which forms the "spine" of the work.

Repeat steps D and E for the desired length. If the loom becomes filled, remove the bar, slide all but the last four loops off the loom, replace the bar, and continue working as before for the desired length.

Afghan Stitch

Figure A

Having made a starting chain in the same manner as for all crochet work, *insert afghan hook into the second chain from the hook, draw up a loop, and repeat from * in each chain across the row, keeping all loops on the hook.

Figure B

Working from left to right, place yarn over the hook and draw it through the first loop on the hook, then *yarn over and draw through two loops, and repeat from * across the row. Chain 1 to turn at the end of the row.

Figure C

Skip the first vertical bar, *insert hook from right to left under the top strand of the next vertical bar, yarn over and draw through a loop, and repeat from * across the row, keeping all loops on the hook and ending by inserting the hook under both strands of the last vertical bar.

Figure D

Work in the same manner as for B.
Steps C and D are repeated throughout for the working of the basic afghan stitch.

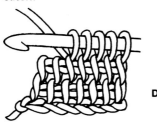

Knitting

Casting On

For your first stitch, make a slip loop on the needle, allowing a two-yard end of yarn for every 100 stitches that are to be cast on, more if the yarn is a heavier-than-average weight and less if it is lighter. Holding the needle in your right hand with the short end of the yarn toward you, *make a loop on your left thumb with the short end (A). Insert the needle from front to back through this loop (B), then place the yarn attached to the ball under and around the needle (C), draw the yarn through the loop, and pull the short end down to tighten it (D). Repeat from * for the desired number of stitches.

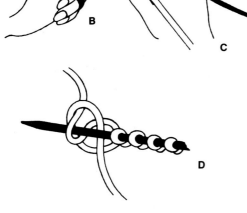

Knitting

Holding the needle with the cast-on stitches in your left hand with the yarn to the back of the work, *insert the needle in your right hand from the left to right through the front of the first stitch, wrap the yarn completely around the right needle to form a loop, slip the needle and loop through the stitch, and then slip the stitch just worked off the left needle. Repeat from * across all the stitches on the left needle.

Purling

*Holding the yarn in front of the work, insert the right needle from right to left through the front of the first stitch on the left needle, wrap the yarn completely around the right needle to form a loop, slip the stitch just worked off the left needle. Repeat from * across all the stitches on the left needle.

Binding Off

Knit the first 2 stitches, *insert the point of the left needle into the first stitch on the right needle (A), lift this stitch over the second stitch, and then drop it off the needle (B). Repeat from * across the necessary number of stitches to be bound off. When all the stitches are to be bound off at the end of a piece of work and just one stitch remains, break off the yarn and draw the remaining strand through the stitch. All binding off should be done very loosely so that there is a sufficient amount of elasticity to the finished edge.

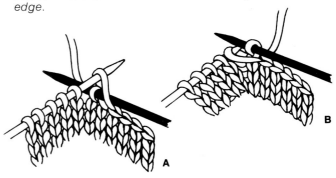

Increasing

Insert the right needle from right to left through the back of the next stitch on the left needle, then wrap the yarn completely around the needle to form a loop (A), slip the needle and loop through to the front (thus forming a new stitch on the right needle), and then knit the same stitch on the left needle in the usual manner (B). Slip the stitch off the left needle.

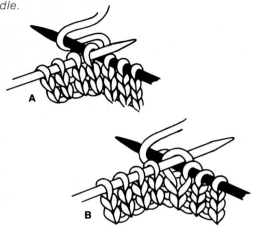

Decreasing

Insert the right needle through 2 stitches on the left needle and work these 2 stitches together as one.

Picking Up Stitches

Picking up stitches—often necessary around a neck or an armhole—is always done on the right side of the work and is usually started at a seam edge, such as the top of one shoulder for neck stitches or at the underarm for an armhole shaping. Stitches are picked up by inserting the right needle through the center of the desired stitch, placing the yarn around the needle, and drawing the yarn and the needle through the stitch, thus forming a new stitch on the right needle. The number of stitches to be picked up on any given piece of work should be distributed evenly so that the work lies flat.

Stockinette Stitch

Perhaps the most basic stitch used in knitting, the stockinette stitch is worked by alternating one row of knit stitches on the right side of the work with one row of purl stitches on the wrong side.

Macramé

Clove Hitch

Tie Half Hitch #1 twice (see Lark's Head).

Diagonal Double Half Hitch

Tie each cord twice around the outermost strand, which is the foundation, as shown.

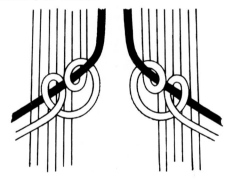

From Right to Left   **From Left to Right**

Double Half Hitch

Fold one strand in half. Place loop over foundation cord and pull ends through.

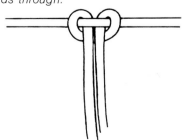

Lark's Head
Tie Half Hitch #1 followed by Half Hitch #2.

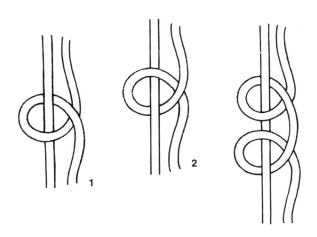

Half Square Knot
Tie, in three steps as illustrated, the first half of the square knot.

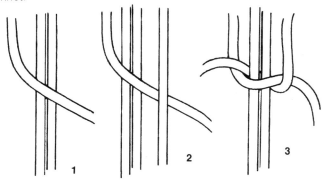

First Half of Knot

Square Knot
Tie the half square knot above followed by the three steps for the second half of the knot below.

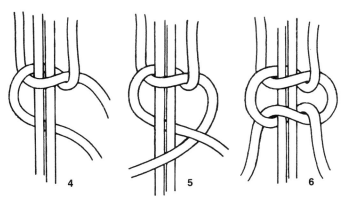

Second Half of Knot

Slip Knot
The simplest knot in all needlework, tie this one as shown.

Windaround Knot
Make this final covering knot by wrapping cord around the completed work and then fastening.

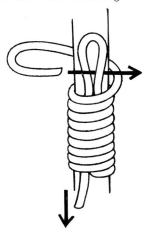

Latchet Hooking

Figure A
Fold a piece of yarn in half over the shank of your hook just below the latch.

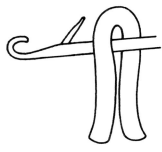

Figure B

Holding the two ends of yarn between the thumb and index finger of your left hand and holding the latch down with the index finger of your right hand, insert the hook under the double horizontal threads of the canvas and then bring it up through the space directly above them, having the latch of the hook in position now above the horizontal threads. Draw the hook slightly toward you until the latch is at a right angle to the shank.

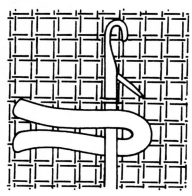

Figure C

Bring the ends of the yarn over the shank of the hook, which is now positioned between the latch and the hooked end.

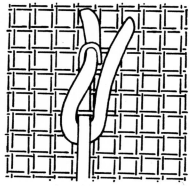

Figure D

Pull the hook through the canvas, drawing the ends of the yarn through the loop.

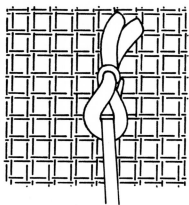

Figure E

Pull the loose ends to tighten the knot.

Needlepoint and Embroidery

Continental Stitch

Beginning at the right edge of the canvas, bring the thread up through point (A), down through point (B), up through point (C), down through point (D), and continue across the row in this way. For the second row, the canvas may be turned upside down and the row worked as the first or the thread may be cut and the next row started again at the right edge.

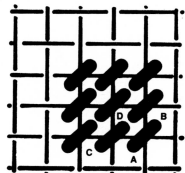

Cross-Stitch

Bring the thread up through the canvas from the wrong to the right side at point (A) and then down from right to wrong side at point (B). Continue working across the canvas in this way for the desired number of stitches. Return across this same row to complete the second part of the crosses by bringing the thread up at point (C) and down at point (D).

French Knot

Bring thread through from wrong to right side of the fabric at point (A) and wrap it around the needle once or as many times as desired. Then pass the needle down through the fabric at point A. The completed stitch should look like Figure 3 below.

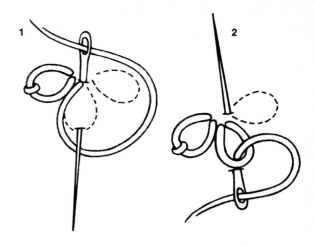

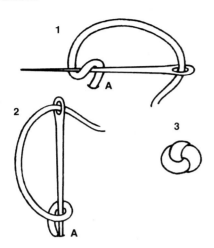

Gobelin Stitch

Working with a little looser tension than normal, bring thread up from wrong to right side at point (A), down at point (B), up at point (C), and down again at point (D). This stitch may be done over any desired number of threads.

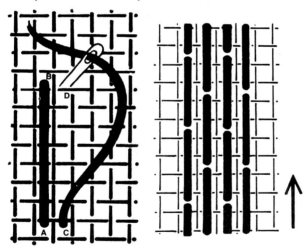

Lazy Daisy or Loop Stitch

Bring the thread through at the base of the petal on the traced line; then loop the thread around the needle and pass the needle back through the fabric, bringing it up at the center top of the petal with the thread under the needle. Make a small stitch over the loop to hold it in place, pass the needle through the fabric, and bring it up at the base of the next petal.

Leaf Stitch

Bring thread up at point (A), down through (B), and continue the stitch in a clockwise manner as shown for each leaf.

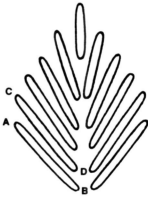

Mosaic Stitch

Bring thread up through point (A), down through point (B), up through point (C), down through point (D), up through point (E), and down through point (F) to complete the first mosaic stitch. Begin the second stitch at point (G) and continue as for the first stitch.

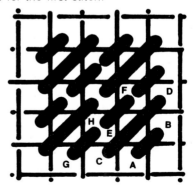

Outline Stitch

Bring the thread through at point (A) on a traced line and then pass the needle through the fabric from (B) to (C). Next, pass the needle through from (D) to (B). Continue working in this manner for the length desired.

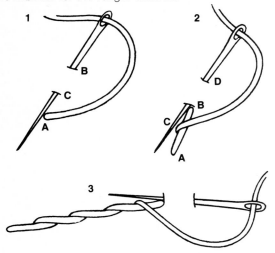

Overcast Stitch

Bring thread through two thicknesses of fabric in one motion, as shown.

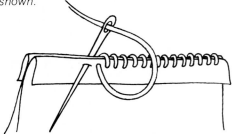

Padded Satin Stitch

Bring thread up vertically through point (A), down through point (B) and continue in this manner to make the base layer of stitches. Cover this layer horizontally by bringing the thread up through point (A) and down at (B) to finish.

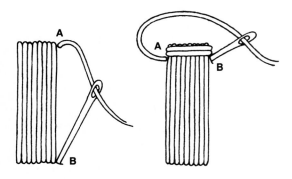

Running Back Stitch

This stitch is worked from right to left along a traced or other established line. Bring the thread up through a given line at any point to be marked (A), pass it through the fabric at (B), and then bring it out again at (C). Continue to work in this manner for the desired length.

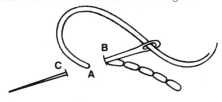

Running Chain Stitch

This stitch is also worked along a traced or other established line. Bring the thread up through a given line at any point to be marked (A), pass the needle through from (A) to (B), and then pull it through. Continue in this manner, passing the needle through from (A) to (B), for the desired length.

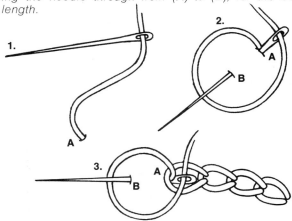

Satin Stitch

Bring the thread through at (A) along any traced or other established line. Then pass the needle down through the fabric at (B) on another established line at the opposite side of the stitch. Carry the needle across the back of the material and pass it through at the point next to (A). Continue to work in the same manner as for the first stitch.

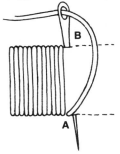

Straight Stitch

Bring thread through at (A) along a traced or other established line and pass the needle through the fabric at (B). Continue to work in this manner.

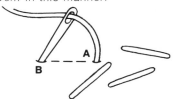

INDEX

Figures in italics refer to illustrations.

ACKNOWLEDGMENTS

The author wishes to compliment the many yarn manufacturers and distributors who have been commendable in their efforts to foster and further the practice of art needlework in our country and also to extend special thanks to those companies listed below who have been most cooperative in furnishing their lovely materials for the purpose of designing the many interesting projects shown on the pages of this book.

Emile Bernat & Sons Co., Uxbridge, Massachusetts
Brunswick Worsted Mills, Inc., Pickens, South Carolina
Coats & Clark, Inc., Stamford, Connecticut
Columbia-Minerva Corporation, New York, New York
Paragon Art & Linen Co., Inc., New York, New York
Reynolds Yarns, Inc., New York, New York
Spinnerin Yarn Co., Inc., New York, New York
William Unger & Co., Inc., New York, New York

Photography Credits
Sports equipment, courtesy of Herman's World of Sporting Goods, 845 Third Ave., New York, N.Y. All plants, courtesy of King Exotic Plants, 774 Avenue of the Americas, New York, N.Y. Wicker chair, bamboo shade, sisil rug, and bird-cage, courtesy of The Wickery, Inc. 342 Third Ave., New York, N.Y. Bentley, courtesy of Unique Motor Cars LTD, 21 East Shore Road, Manhasset, L.I.

cover photograph: John Garetti

color photography:
    art director—Keith Sheridan
    photographer—Arthur Westphal
    stylist—Christine Witko

illustrations: Carol Hines

black and white photography: John Garetti